MW01686925

pushing the beach

The troller *Lyra* fishing around Cape Scott at the northern tip of Vancouver Island. Note the trolling poles are lowered into position. *(Photo reproduction by Nicole Brown Photography, of an oil painting by Mary Russell)*

PUSHING the BEACH

The Story of Marine Link Transportation and the MV Aurora Explorer

Alan H. Meadows

with S.C. Heal

ALAN H. MEADOWS
Victoria, BC

CORDILLERA LEGACY BOOKS
Vancouver, BC

Cover Design by Ten Plus Productions, New Westminster, BC
Cover Photo: *Aurora Explorer* underway in Johnstone Strait with a full cargo deck.
(Alan Meadows photo)
Photo Credits: Unless specified otherwise, all photographs are from the Alan Meadows collection.
Book Layout and Design by Jean Robinson, Victoria, BC
Illustrations:
Frontispiece: The troller *Lyra:*
Original oil painting by Mary Russell, Coal Harbour, BC, 1984.
Photo reproduction by Nicole Brown Photography, Victoria, BC
Maps:
Operational Area of mv *Aurora Explorer* (pp. 154–55):
Marine Link Tours
Fold-out Map: The Delivery Voyage of mv *Aurora Explorer:*
Denton Pendergast, Rocket Science Design, Victoria, BC
Printed and Bound in Canada by Friesens, Altona, MB

Library and Archives Canada Cataloguing in Publication

Meadows, Alan H., 1948-, author
Pushing the beach : the story of Marine Link Transportation and the MV Aurora Explorer / Alan H. Meadows with S.C. Heal.

Includes index.
ISBN 978-0-9948788-0-9 (paperback)

1. Marine Link Transportation--History. 2. Aurora Explorer (Ship)--History. 3. Freight and freightage--British Columbia--History. 4. Cargo ships--British Columbia--Passenger traffic--History. I. Title.

HE597.C2M43 2015 387.506'5711 C2015-90627

PUBLISHED BY:
Alan H. Meadows
ahm@shaw.ca

WITH THE ASSISTANCE OF:
Cordillera Legacy Books
102 - 8708 French St
Vancouver, BC V6P 4W7
604-261-1695
richbook@telus.net

MIX
Paper from responsible sources
FSC® C016245
www.fsc.org

TO
HOLLY MEADOWS
Ever my rock and safe harbour through life.

TO
JUDY CAMPBELL
Forever to be known as Mrs. Marine Link.

TO
THE MEMORY OF PETER C. THOMSON
Founder of Trotac Marine Supply, Victoria, BC.
Business mentor and long-time friend.
Greatly missed.

ACKNOWLEDGEMENTS

This book has been five years in the making. There were times when I felt overwhelmed with having to recall details over a forty-five year period. Just getting the chronology of events correct has proved daunting.

Every effort has been made to minimize errors and deficiencies and I thank the following people for proofreading the manuscript:

Mike Pinch, Laurie McBride, Tim Campbell, Guy Adams, Tom Brown, John and David Hitchcock, Mike Walden, John Sanderson and Al Chambers.

Thank you to Denton Pendergast of Rocket Science Design for his production of the map of the *Aurora Explorer*'s voyage from Fort McMurray to Campbell River. *(see fold-out map)*

Thank you to Bill Clarke of Helifor Industries and to Ford Cannon of Marine Link for helping to track down various photographs.

Thank you also to the team at Cordillera Books: Tamara Sale, for the cover design; Audrey Scammell, typist extraordinaire; and especially, Jean Robinson, for book layout and design, editing, proofing and much more.

And most of all, my thanks to Syd Heal for his patience and encouragement, without which this book would not have been published.

Alan H. Meadows

CONTENTS

PREFACE

Many people have influenced my life and contributed to the success I have enjoyed. My life has been enriched by many mentors on my journey as an entrepreneur and I have benefitted from their knowledge and wisdom. Many are named in the text, particularly my partners and staff at Marine Link Transportation Ltd. and Campbell River Marine Terminal Ltd., but I would specifically like to recognize the following:

Foremost, my late father, Richard **'Dick' Meadows,** former naval officer and marine surveyor. Dad took immense pride in Marine Link and was always there when we needed help or advice.

John Hitchcock, a guiding light in Forest & Marine Financial Corporation. It is a privilege to have known and worked with him through key transactions that made Marine Link Transportation the success that it is.

The late **Tom Kenny** of Victoria, former Chief Petty Officer in the RCN and "master fixer," whose guidance in my early days of commercial fishing was of enormous value.

The late **Frank James,** who got me on a horse and shared his life experiences as we explored the Chilcotin landscape from his cabin at Beaverdam Lake.

Ken Olding, production manager at Oakland Industries, the fish processing plant in Victoria Harbour, and then part-owner of SSI Sea Products Ltd. in Ganges, Saltspring Island. With co-owner **John Christenson** they entrusted me with upwards of $750,000 cash to go out and buy roe herring on the fishing grounds. Ken was always there as a true friend and still is today.

Grant Little, a chance meeting in a sports store evolved into a thirty-five-year friendship. I have been the grateful recipient of Grant's help in financial and insurance matters.

Mike Walden, lawyer, now retired, always available with sound advice for over twenty-five years. The clock stopped when the camaraderie took over and I never received a bill that I considered to be out of line. Mike also took the time to read the final draft of this book to ensure that we had not put our collective feet in our mouths, from a legal standpoint.

Wayne Clark and **Blaine Wright,** who taught me much about sales and selling while aboard *Powder Hound II.*

The late **Peter C. Thomson** (or "PC" and "AH" as we commonly greeted each other), who together with wife Chris and son Campbell built their own business, Trotac Marine Supply, from the floor up. If I ever needed ultra-conservative, yet sound, business advice, PC was there to give it.

John Sanderson, whose repartee about life, politics and business and much more was a delight to participate in.

John Hurley, an extraordinary craftsman who could fix or build anything.

Steve Shewchuk, who gave a lost young man a seat in the barber shop and many talks about life which, looking back, gave me needed direction from which, as Steve recently commented, "I never looked back."

The late **Henry Frew,** who more than any other influenced my direction in both business and life. A journalist and publisher, Henry was always ready to debate in such a way that it forced one to be capable of thinking "outside the box."

Mike Pinch, chartered accountant, a solid friend and long-term assistant and sometime deckhand, who has provided a valuable sounding board to me for the past thirty years.

Alan Chambers, RPF (Registered Professional Forester) and extraordinary thinker. An academic who exhibits an abundance of common sense and practical application. Al built his own troller in his backyard on West Sixth Street in Vancouver and fished it for thirteen years out of Bamfield on the west coast of Vancouver Island. This was his preference, instead of publishing papers looking for academic kudos.

The late **Don Cruikshank,** CEO and part owner of Seafood Products Ltd., Port Hardy, BC. Another immensely intelligent yet down-to-earth and articulate personality. His door was always open to me, to my great benefit.

The late **Jack Brook**s of Sooke, BC, a simple fisheries guardian but the most "connected to nature" individual I have ever known. Jack and I spent much time together from which I learned to look much closer when dealing with natural surroundings. A gem of a man.

Tom Brown, my relative and supporter—always there, always positive.

Alan H. Meadows

Amphibious operations in the retaking of Malaya in 1945. In this beach scene at Morib, a small Vehicle Landing Craft (LCV) is in the left foreground. *(S.C. Heal collection)*

A beached Tank Landing Craft (LCT) awaits the rising tide on a beach at Morib, Malaya. *(S.C. Heal)*

INTRODUCTION

The Marine Link story is one of incredible perseverance. Alan Meadows established a fledgling business and was joined shortly after by Tim Campbell. It involved the collection and purchase of roe herring for the export market. It was a free-enterprise operation that incorporated the best elements of a Horatio Alger story—two young fishermen, each owning their own boat, saw the writing on the wall for the fishing industry and decided to strike out in a new direction. Naturally, the business had its ups and downs, and while the partners readily admit to mistakes, none were fatal and most carried an important lesson with them.

MLT was formally incorporated in 1979. Since then the company has owned four self-propelled landing craft-type vessels, including the current flagship *Aurora Explorer,* an unusual vessel based on the lines of war-time navy, ramp-equipped, tank-landing vessels. They are loaded with heavy mobile equipment and all manner of merchandise from live fish to groceries to aviation fuel and explosives which they deliver to the beaches and docks along the BC coast. Twelve fare-paying passengers on the *Aurora* experience life aboard a working freight vessel, watching with rapt attention as the crew handles the cargo.

Some years ago I took my first trip aboard the *Aurora Explorer.* As I watched her operations, memories were rekindled of wartime amphibious operations when LCTs, LCIs and smaller LCMs and LCVs delivered troops, tanks, artillery vehicles and supplies to enemy-held shorelines in Europe, Africa and Asia during WWII. During those war years, I gained ship-handling experience as a serving sailor. These vessel types have always intrigued me.

In 1991 Al and Tim were joined by Guy Adams, another former troll salmon fisherman, who gained experience afloat in the MLT vessels and then came ashore as the dispatcher. In 2006 Guy purchased MLT and its most important source of income, the *Aurora Explorer.* He is continuing the same freight boat tradition as his predecessors, handling cargo and providing tasteful and comfortable accommodation for the passengers. He continues the same tradition of excellence: service, wholesome food, a friendly, safety-conscious crew and a bridge where passengers are always welcome.

Al and Tim have not fully retired, remaining active in the affairs of Campbell River Marine Terminal (CRMT) which is engaged in the ongoing development of a full-service marine terminal at Menzies Bay, 15 km (9 mi) north of Campbell River, BC. It provides a home base for Marine Link Transportation, owner of the *Aurora Explorer,* as well as other tenants and local marine operators.

One might ask, Why this book? Why the story of Marine Link, its three principal personalities and the many others who have contributed over a forty-year period? One reason is because it is an account of human achievement and the development of a successful and vital BC coastal business enterprise.

Al tells the story openly and honestly, in layman's language, lumps and all. It includes experiences dealing with unhelpful bankers and professional advisors who did not measure up. It touches on the many issues surrounding ship ownership and finance, marine insurance, dealing with crews and staff, naval architects and shipyards and the challenges of ship operations from calculating the viability of new services and major items of expenditure. In short, while it is essentially a corporate history and personal biography, it is also a business study of a major BC industry.

Marine transportation is the more commonly used label for BC coastal towing and shipping companies. These ship owning and operating enterprises are faced with the same decisions as the largest deep-sea shipping company. The differences are in the details, relative sizes and issues of scale. Marine transportation businesses seldom stand still for long, and if they do it usually indicates a stagnant market or uninspired management.

The Marine Link story is one of inspired leadership, street smarts born of experience and common sense, vision, a willingness to take risks and determination to achieve success. There is also a skill in avoiding rash decisions that can lead to corporate ruin. Marine Link Transportation and its associated companies have demonstrated their survivorship skills over forty years of active business. With the founder Alan Meadows now easing out of the business for health reasons, a new generation is taking over. It is the perfect time to tell their unique story.

S.C. Heal

ORIGIN OF THE TITLE "PUSHING THE BEACH"

(by Syd Heal)

During WWII specialized vessels were built for amphibious landings. Commonly known by their initials with an attached number, the basic landing craft were:

- LCT - landing craft for tanks, large guns and heavy vehicles;
- LCI - landing craft for infantry;
- LCM - landing craft for a mechanized single truck or light armoured vehicle;
- LCV - with a similar purpose to an LCM in carrying a light vehicle or for carrying personnel, but smaller and handier;
- LCA - small landing craft used in an assault on a beach; being fast and small they could dart in, disembark about 40 troops with all their gear and be back on their way to the mother LSI within a very short period of time.

LCT and LCI were fully capable of undertaking long-distance ocean voyages, usually in a group with an escort ship like a destroyer or frigate. The smaller LCM, LCV and LCA were carried lift-on, lift-off style aboard freighters and LSI, the large infantry landing ships, developed from converted freighters. In many theatres of war, loaded landing craft were sometimes required to go into a beach and with engines set at "half ahead" or "slow ahead" depending on tidal and weather conditions, the vessel would literally "push the beach" while discharging her cargo. As many beaches were sometimes extended as shallow water well out to sea, the larger LCTs and LCIs were fitted with large capstans at their sterns with a direct power take-off from the engines below. When the vessel was going into the beach a kedge anchor was dropped into the sea and a wire line paid out. When the vessel had completed off-loading and was lighter, the capstan astern was started up as she hauled herself off the beach on the wire anchor line and the vessel was helped to return to deep water.

Exactly the same routine is followed on the BC coast except that the kedge anchor is not usually fitted to our coastal landing craft as most landings are over steeply shelving small beaches. Otherwise the practice of pushing the beach is exactly the same as that employed by the war-time landing craft and is the inspiration for the title of this book.

The *Aurora Explorer* is an LCT type of landing craft.

The *Lyra* when I bought her in 1971, showing her original colours. Note the trolling poles are up in the crosstree. *(John Homer photo)*

Chapter 1

THE BEGINNING

MY EARLY YEARS AS A COMMERCIAL FISHERMAN

I graduated from Victoria High School in 1966 and then started at the University of Victoria, which was in its infancy at that time. I was not really interested in what university held for me and I essentially warmed a seat for two years. I also spent a lot of time mulling my future while visiting with Steve Shewchuk at his barbershop in the Cedar Hill area of Victoria. Steve was instrumental in giving my life some direction, pointing me toward my first job in commercial fishing, as a deckhand for Fred Barber on his troller, the *Jean B.* The deckhand on a troller (typically a two- or three-person crew) was expected to pull gear, land fish, dress fish out and ice them down in the hold below and, on occasion, cook.

In my next fishing season I switched boats and joined Dick Williams on his troller, the *Seabeam,* for two seasons, 1970 and 1971. Occasionally, the *Seabeam* would unload a ten- to twelve-day trip at the Oakland Industries fish processing plant in Victoria. At the time, Oakland Industries was located at the foot of Yates Street next to the Johnson Street Bridge. It later moved to a new and larger facility in the harbour which today is a series of condominium buildings on Montreal Street.

After deckhanding for three years on the *Jean B* and the *Seabeam,* I bought my own west coast troller late in 1971, the *Lyra.*

THE BEST OF TIMES

The 1970s was a delightful time to be in the commercial fishing industry. I was not a "highliner" but I did catch my share and managed to pay off the purchase of the *Lyra* relatively quickly. Commercial salmon trolling was one of those occupations that you got out of it what you put into it. The old adage that 20 percent of the fishermen caught 80 percent of the fish was true. However, this coast-wide fleet of some 2,500 trollers supported the economies of outports on the west coast of Vancouver Island and the Queen Charlotte Islands. These included such communities as Sooke, Bamfield, Ucluelet, Tofino, Port Hardy, Port Alberni, Kyuquot, Winter Harbour, Sointula, Alert Bay, Queen Charlotte City, Masset and Prince Rupert. If the fishing season was not terribly successful then you went hand-logging or beachcombing or some other such activity in the off-season.

Trolling was the sector of the fishery that

Al in the cockpit of the *Lyra* landing salmon into the checkers, lower left.

THE LYRA

The *Lyra* was a typical west coast troller, 40' in length and 13' in beam, and usually operated with a crew of two or three. The boat was built of wood in 1948 by Matsumoto Shipyard in North Vancouver. Named after the star constellation Lyra in the southern hemisphere, *Lyra* had two sister ships. The vessel was distinguished by being a superb sea boat and very stable to work on, even in high wave and wind conditions. The *Lyra* was what was known as an ice packer, which meant that at the beginning of each trip six tons of flake ice was loaded into the hold. The fish caught were iced down three or four times a day over as much as a twelve-day trip with the ice keeping the fish in good condition.

attracted individuals who wanted an independent lifestyle or occupation. The participants in the fishery were very diverse—just within the Victoria troll fleet alone, some 250 boats, there were former police officers, university professors, an Olympic silver medalist, a former vice-president of Zellers stores, a former physicist, engineers, bush pilots and other diverse backgrounds.

Of the three commercial gear types for fishing salmon—hook and line trolling, seine netting and gillnetting—trolling was the choice of the independent owner/operator. It was hard work, often in bad weather, sometimes as much as 50–70 miles (80–113 km) offshore. If the weather was too tough, you either jogged in, sometimes taking days, or anchored if the depth of water allowed. If those weren't options, you simply drifted at the end of your parachute/sea anchor and waited for the weather to go down. Regardless, you were your own fixer if things went wrong and therefore trolling attracted the most self-sufficient people.

The salmon fisheries of BC started around 1880 and consisted of small gill-netters operating in open boats powered by sail or oars. The fishery was largely confined to major river estuaries and their immediate approaches. Examples of these were the Fraser River, the major rivers emptying into Rivers Inlet in the midcoast and the Skeena and Nass Rivers near Prince Rupert. By far the greater tonnages of salmon are landed by the net fisheries, primarily by the highly mechanized drum seiners. As the industry grew through the 1950s and 1960s, there were challenges in terms of fleet size and catch taken. There were numerous canneries up and down the BC coast and these were the economic drivers that, along with logging, sustained many coastal communities and its hinterland people.

DO NOT CONFUSE TROLLERS WITH TRAWLERS

Seiners, gillnetters, trollers and trawlers are engaged in fishing for the different species of fin fish on the BC coast. Drum seiners are the large boats that fish with a seine net which literally encircles a school of fish. When the fish are entrapped, the net is pursed up much like a drawstring bag. The fish are scooped with a brailer, essentially a large dip net.

Gillnetters are smaller boats, most commonly found in estuarial areas like the Fraser and Skeena Rivers and in Johnstone and Queen Charlotte Straits. They fish with a gillnet, sized to catch salmon by the gills as the fish attempts to get through the precisely sized web. Therefore, the application describes the boat. Gillnetters are believed to have originated in Western Europe where they were used for fishing in rivers.

A troller is a vessel that fishes with hooked lures and runs several main lines from each side of the boat. The most common species taken is salmon. Lures are clipped to these main lines, sometimes numbering between twenty and three hundred lures, depending on the type of salmon being targeted. The boat pulls these hooked lures through the water at a fast walking speed and as the fish bite a bell rings up on the trolling pole on either side of the boat. *(see frontispiece photo of the* Lyra*)* The name is believed to have originated in Norway where a national symbol is the small wooden troll or doll, usually hand carved and given as a good luck charm to sailors and fishermen. Prior to WWI, a large number of Scandinavian and Yugoslavian immigrant fishermen settled into the BC fisheries and brought their fishing skills with them. Trollers were often referred to as "swivel necks" because they would swivel their heads from side to side waiting and watching for the bells on the poles to ring.

The distinguishing features of a troller are the long poles (typically 40'–50' long of either aluminum or wood) which, when fishing, are lowered at a 45° angle off the side of the boat. *(see frontispiece)* In the case of the *Lyra,* two bow poles are also featured. These poles are configured in this way and help keep the main lines, to which the lures are clipped, spaced apart. When not in use the poles are pulled up to a vertical position and housed in the crosstree of the boat's mast. *(see p.xiv)*

A trawler is a larger vessel, usually having a crew of four to six, which pulls a wide-mouthed net in the shape of a large bag. These scoop up bottom and midwater fish such as sole, cod, flounder, brill and hake. A trawl net can be highly productive but can also be very destructive of the bottom and environment of smaller fish. The trawler was of British-German-Dutch origin and used in many worldwide fisheries such as the deep North Atlantic waters off the Grand Banks of Newfoundland and Iceland. In BC, trawlers are usually referred to as "draggers" given their method of fish harvesting.

A SEA ANCHOR

A sea anchor is an amazing piece of gear. It is actually a parachute, of the same type and size that you would use to jump out of an airplane. Care had to be taken when setting it out over the bow of the boat because the wind could catch it before it was fully deployed in the water. Boats were observed chasing their parachute high up and ahead of the boat in full blossom, but once in the water the parachute opened up. The lead rope back to the boat was often well over 200' consisting of 5/8" braided nylon which led into a small bridle over the bow and a tie-up point on the boat's bow cleat or anchor winch. This kept the bow of the boat nicely into the wind and waves even if it was a screaming storm. The magic of this set up was that the rope stretched and the parachute fell back in the waves giving the boat a very comfortable and safe situation to ride out the bad weather.

THE HERRING FISHERY

The history of the herring fishery was similar to that of the salmon. Its pursuit in the early days was based on greed, with heavy exploitation of the vast schools returning to spawn. Herring are recognized as perhaps the single-most important element in the marine food chain, along with other fish such as sardines, oolichans, sand lance and mackerel. Herring are at the very foundation of the resource, the prime source of food for all our Pacific species of salmon, except sockeye which are zoo-plankton feeders. Therefore, as the herring decline so can the stocks of some species of salmon. Typically in the past, herring were processed for their oil and meal value with a small percentage retained for human consumption.

Through the 1950s and 1960s, the west coast herring stocks were overfished by the seine-boat sector, culminating in the fishery being closed entirely in 1968 until 1975. As a result of that closure, herring stocks have recovered in most parts of the coast, but they still remain vulnerable to overfishing.

Today, the old canning companies are almost extinct and a new generation of fresh fish processors has taken their place. The modern BC fisherman has to go further afield to make a living and looks at other fisheries such as the trapping of sablefish, prawns and crab, the longlining of halibut and dogfish and the offshore fishing of tuna.

Fortunately, there have been new opportunities. One of these is the roe herring fishery which began in the mid-1970s as the result of an emerging specialty market in Japan known as "kazunoko."

The reduction of herring for fishmeal and oil was not sustainable, but this new niche market created a small controlled fishery for the extraction of roe from mature herring.

Probably the foremost fish eaters in the world are the Japanese and Scandinavians. The Japanese especially value the skeins of roe found in the mature female herring as well as herring "spat" or eggs that set on kelp. In some years the annual spatfall of herring roe was so huge that much of it set on rocks and pilings. It looked almost like a cream-coloured snow at low tide, exposing the rubbery layers of spawn which quickly died when it was exposed to sunlight and the atmosphere.

Today, the major stocks and largest body of herring migrate into and out of the Strait of Georgia during December through April each year. A herring spawning is typified by the fish moving into shallow waters and laying its eggs on eel grass or kelp in what appears to be milky green water. Seals, sea lions and all manner of seabird life take part in the feast.

This emerging small gillnet fishery at first targeted localized areas in Ganges Bay and Long Harbour on Saltspring Island. Foremost in developing this new fishery was John Christenson of SSI Sea Products Ltd., a small fish processing plant in the town of Ganges.

Al is helping unload a skiff full of herring. "Where there's muck there's money."[1] (circa 1979)

1. A statement famously quoted by W.A.C. Bennett, premier of BC, 1952–1972.

KAZUNOKO

At the outset, this new fishery's harvest was less than 1,000 tons coast-wide and was targeted for a very specific market in Japan. This was the high-end boutique gift known as "kazunoko"; in their culture the Japanese, particularly in the business world, have a tradition of exchanging high-priced gifts. The process of producing kazunoko involves removing the skein of eggs from the female herring after it has been frozen or brined. The carcasses of the intact male herring and those of the female, with eggs removed at the end of the process, are sent to a rendering plant for the production of fish meal. The export of herring roe for this market grew exponentially in value in the late 1970s. It was a single-customer market with all the inherent risks that brings. Since the Japanese economy tanked some twenty years ago the kazunoko market has steadily declined.

ALASKA BLACK COD

So you have ordered smoked Alaska black cod for your dining out dinner. I would too as it is one of my favourites, very rich and flavourful. But hold on a minute, there are a few things you might want to know about the choice you have made. First off, it is sablefish and not black cod that you will be eating. And it is not caught in Alaska but right here off the West Coast of Vancouver Island and the Queen Charlotte Islands, out in very deep water. And it is a white-fleshed fish where processors (some, not all) dye the flesh red with food colouring because the consumer will buy a "red-fleshed" fish more readily over that of a white fish. And then there is the "smoke" which is often introduced in the form of artificial "chemical" smoke. The consumer can still find fish stores where none of this falsification and misleading marketing takes place—so know what to ask for.

The *Lyra* with new colours tied up at Fisherman's Wharf, Victoria, BC. Note the heavy-duty Northill anchor on the bow. Most trollers had very heavy anchor gear providing the ability to anchor in very deep water. (circa 1975)

Chapter 2

MARINE LINK TRANSPORTATION LTD.

THE BEGINNING OF A LIFE-LONG FRIENDSHIP

The Marine Link story begins with a new friendship in the spring of 1970, on my first trip as deckhand on the *Seabeam.* We had completed unloading our catch at Oakland Industries in Victoria when a face peered down from the piling dock high above and a voice complimented me on a job well done dressing the fish we had just delivered. The face and voice belonged to Ken Olding, the production manager for Oakland Industries. That chance meeting with Ken would lead to an amazing life experience.

Ken Olding, formerly the production manager at Oakland Industries. He joined John Christenson at SSI Sea Products Ltd. on Saltspring Island in 1976. Ken and I are of like mind. Our friendship endures to this day.

Ken left Oakland Industries in 1976 and joined John Christenson as partners in SSI Sea Products Ltd. in Ganges on Saltspring Island. In the fall of 1976 he contacted me to see if I would be interested in doing some commission buying and packing of herring for their company.

I was intrigued and interested in his proposal and set about finding the equipment and manpower necessary to do the job. At this time the small roe herring fishery took place along the shorelines of the lower Gulf Islands and Strait of Georgia. The volume of herring harvested was very modest and the equipment we needed for this first year's undertaking was primarily a flatdeck truck equipped with a crane. I secured this from Budget Rent A Truck and I hired a friend to help. Peter Kennedy joined me in Ganges, bringing his camper truck which served as our office/accommodation for about three weeks in the spring of 1977. We first set up to buy roe herring from fishermen operating in Ganges Bay and Long Harbour, located on the lower end of Saltspring Island. At that

A Budget rental hoist truck, similar to the one Pete Kennedy and I used when we bought roe herring that first year.

Pete Kennedy worked with me in the 1977 roe herring fishery. Later he worked as a deckhand and cook on the *Georgia Transporter*.

The concrete boat ramp at French Creek where Pete and I bought roe herring.

time the roe herring season began in late February and continued through early March in the Gulf Islands and then moved northwards into the Strait of Georgia.

The crane truck was first set up on the government dock in Ganges and the process of purchasing and unloading got underway. The boom was swung down to lift the brailers full of herring out of the skiff and then swung up and over the cab to unload into tote boxes on the truck's deck. In this process a large dial-scale showed the weight, less that of the aluminum brailer. We positioned eight tote boxes on the deck of the truck, each capable of holding 1800 pounds (816.5 kg) of herring which, once loaded, were transferred to a larger flatdeck semi-trailer truck for delivery to the plant in Ganges.

In early March the fishery shifted northwards in the Strait of Georgia to the area encompassing the east coast of Vancouver Island from Nanoose Bay to Campbell River. We took up station on the concrete boat ramp at French Creek just north of Parksville. Again, the loaded skiffs of herring would come into the boat ramp and we would swing the crane out and carry on with the process of unloading the skiffs.

Once all the totes were full we would back the truck up and transfer the full boxes onto a semi-trailer truck. In that first season Pete Kennedy and I purchased about seventy-five tons of roe herring.

In the 1977 fishery it was a "cash-on-the-spot" payment operation and twice I ran out of money. Picture my wife Holly, eight-months pregnant with our first child, going to the CIBC bank in Parksville and bringing back $40,000 cash in a laundry hamper. The second time I needed even more money and I personally went to the CIBC in Parksville, presented my credentials and asked for $60,000 in cash. After my credentials were checked and rechecked through several layers of bank bureaucracy, I was informed that the bank did not have that much cash on hand and would I come back at closing time. Paint another picture, with myself wearing rubber boots, generously covered with herring scales and I not smelling too fresh either, sitting in the bank vault with two tellers and a supervisor, counting and recounting $60,000. This was a portent of many more surreal events to come.

THERE HAD TO BE A BETTER WAY

This roe herring packing business was backbreaking work, slow and cumbersome, but we learned from it. Following that first season I came away with the conclusion that there had to be a better way to do this. My intuitive solution was to find a landing-craft vessel which could go directly onto the fishing grounds and buy from the fishermen right at their nets. Again, the fish we bought

Georgia Transporter, an early landing craft in the Strait of Georgia. She was built in 1963 by Syd Heal and his colleagues at Georgia Shipping. She has gone through two major late-life rebuilds and is still active today with Island Tug & Barge Ltd., based in Vancouver. *(Rod Logan photo)*

would be loaded into tote boxes but, with a landing craft operating close to boat ramps and docks, the full boxes could be swiftly off-loaded onto flatdeck trucks and the boat would be back on the grounds ready to purchase more fish in hours. Compare this to the traditional fish packer that, once loaded with fish, would set off for Prince Rupert or Vancouver Harbours, unload and turn around, and not reappear on the fishing grounds for five or six days.

At the conclusion of the 1977 fishery I resolved to find a landing craft suitable for this purpose. Initially, my search led me to a number of post-WWII landing craft-type vessels of the LCM configuration *(see p.xiii)* in Tacoma, Washington. Unfortunately, they were unsuitable as they were of relatively light construction and monstrous horsepower, designed for amphibious wartime use and a single trip onto a beach.

I was more successful tracking down a small former Canadian Coast Guard (CCG) landing craft that had been declared surplus and sold to a logging outfit on Ootsa Lake near Smithers, BC. I travelled there to check out this vessel, at the time named Togian. It was being used by the logging operation to move light equipment over the lake during the spring and summer and was up for sale. The *Togian* was 34' in length and 12' in beam and could carry the equivalent of one pickup truck. I immediately recognized its potential and purchased it on the spot.

After I returned to Victoria, I engaged the services of John Jenkins of Jenkins Marine to assist in trailering the *Togian* from Ootsa Lake to Victoria in the winter of 1978. This was most challenging as we had to travel across one arm of frozen Ootsa Lake. During the winter freeze-up, stockpiled logs were hauled across an ice bridge[1] constructed over this arm of the lake. With some trepidation John and I safely made the journey across the ice and with myself as the pilot car we managed to trailer the boat down through the Fraser Canyon to Tsawwassen where it was loaded aboard a BC ferry for Swartz Bay.

Interestingly enough, when we rolled onto the lower car deck of the ferry some of the ferry crew gathered to have a look at the *Togian.* I remember overhearing one of them say, "It has been a while since I have seen one of those." This struck a chord in me as I realized this could only have been uttered by a veteran and somebody who had probably ridden in a landing craft onto an enemy-held beachhead in wartime. *(see p.x)*

Our destination was K&K Kustom Metal located on David Street in Victoria, owned and operated by Ray Sauriol. In the next month, K&K fitted the *Togian* with an enclosed wheelhouse superstructure. They widened her with sponsons full-length and full-depth which increased the beam of the boat to 15'6" and added a hydraulic lifting boom to enable over-the-side loading and unloading.

We needed to change the name from "Togian" to one that would easily identify our business. The question was put to some family members and Holly's mother, Esther

1.The technique of constructing an ice bridge required the builder to bore through the ice and bring water up to flood the surface. This formed a layer of new ice, increasing the thickness of the ice that was a part of the desired roadway. This was repeated until the necessary thickness of ice was reached. In sub-zero weather it did not take long before the thickness of the ice was built up and strengthened enough to allow heavily loaded vehicles to cross. This ice bridge would last until the spring thaw.

The *Togian* is loaded onto John Jenkins' boat trailer at Ootsa Lake, BC. (1978)

Webb, came up with the name "Marine Link." We all recognized immediately that the name had some cachet and it is one that is easily remembered. This name change for our first boat proved to be the core element for the company that emerged shortly after, Marine Link Transportation Ltd. (MLT).

Away we went with this new and improved *Togian*, now the *Marine Link #I (ML#I),* to purchase herring for SSI Sea Products Ltd. The concept of using a landing craft proved to be the right strategy. In the 1978 season we bought substantially more herring using boat ramps at Beachcomber Marina in Northwest Bay and French Creek. We also came to the realization that, even though the concept of a roll-on/roll-off landing craft worked, the boat was really too small.

So at the end of that packing season we returned again to K&K Kustom Metal. We engaged Ron Thicke, a naval architect in North Vancouver, to work up drawings for

Esther Webb.

lengthening the boat. These plans were required to pass Transport Canada Ship Safety certification. Alex Grieg, the senior ship safety officer of Transport Canada in Victoria, was most helpful during this process. The *ML#I* was lengthened by cutting the hull in two transversely and adding a new 20' midsection. When completed, we had a new boat, 54' in length with a 15'6" beam. The reconstructed vessel could now carry upwards of 18 tons of freight.

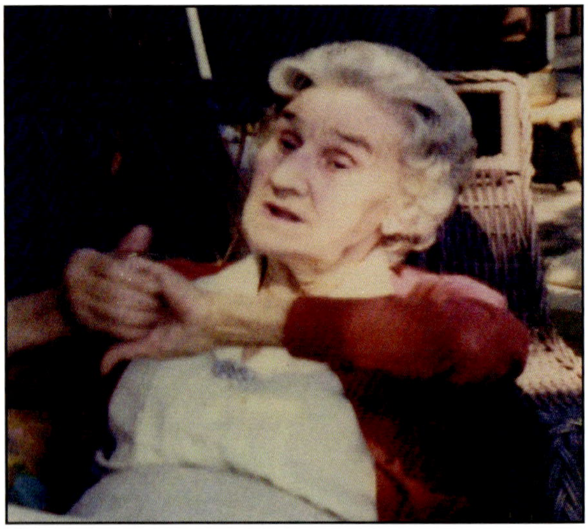

Mrs. Wetmore, who introduced me to Tim.

A NEW PARTNERSHIP AND A NEW BUSINESS VENTURE: MARINE LINK TRANSPORTATION

Perhaps the most significant event in the history of Marine Link Transportation took place in 1978. A mutual friend who lived in Central Saanich (near Victoria) introduced me to a Mrs. Wetmore. She was a widow who lived on Cromar Road near Sidney, BC. She and her husband had operated the Marshall Wells supply boat on the BC coast during the 1950s and 1960s. This grand old lady recognized my involvement with fishing and the sea and invited me to dinner. Also invited was another young man, Tim Campbell. Mrs. Wetmore had obviously recognized kindred spirits.

Tim was a "flatlander" who grew up on a ranch in the foothills of the Alberta Rockies. The family gave up on ranching and moved to Sidney, BC. Tim went to sea as a seaman aboard a number of deep-sea freighters. In the meantime, Tim's dad, Gray Campbell, started a book publishing business, Gray's Publishing. After he returned from sea, Tim worked in the business with his dad for about eight years.

After our introduction, Tim came out for three trips on the *Lyra* as my deckhand and then went off on an albacore tuna fishing schooner, venturing as far away as Hawaii. When *ML#I* came on stream in 1978 I invited Tim to join me in operating the vessel during the roe herring fishery.

The partnership blossomed from the beginning. Each of us has strengths and abilities that the other does not have, at least not to the same degree, and therefore we complement each other. Tim has always been a practical "hands-on, day-to-day" type with a propensity for organizing and building almost anything. He is a man of lists who makes up lists to keep track of his lists—a superb detail person always making sure that things stay on track and remain efficient. Tim is the only person I have ever known who brings a piece of equipment back in better condition than when you gave it to him. His middle name should be "Efficiency"!

Tim might never describe himself as a businessman, yet he has the sort of facile mind that enables him to understand a business deal or arrangement very quickly. I on the other hand am a "big picture person," less interested in the details, but possessing reasonable business and financial management skills. I have a "radar" that is good at looking over the horizon.

Only a few business partnerships last this length of time, but thanks to Mrs. Wetmore our introduction resulted in a forty-year-old team that continues to this day. In part this book is a celebration of this very successful partnership.

Over the years, *ML#I* proved to be a hardy and durable workhorse on the coast. Marine Link Transportation sold *ML#I* to Stolt Sea Farms in 1996; they renamed her "Kaso." She is still active today.

ONE OF MANY LESSONS LEARNED

The major logistical challenge of operating *ML#I* was where to "land the landing craft." During the 1978 roe herring fishery in the Strait of Georgia, we used the boat launching ramp at Beachcomber Marina in Northwest Bay. Here we off-loaded the boxed herring, with the aid of a forklift, onto large semi-trailer trucks for transport to Ganges. While we were unloading one night, Tim and I failed to adequately monitor the tide, which was dropping quickly. To our chagrin, the *ML#I* became stranded on the boat ramp. To make matters worse, our vigorous attempts to move

Tim Campbell and I on the beach in front of *ML#I*. The boat had just come out of the K&K Kustom Metal shop for the first time. A lifting boom apparatus and wheelhouse have been added. (circa 1978)

the boat off by going full astern resulted in a nearby submerged boulder, about eight inches in diameter, being sucked into the propeller cage. The aluminum propeller was instantly demolished.

There we sat, fully out of the water, at low tide, stranded high and dry at two o'clock on a very dark morning. Even if the tide came in and refloated the boat, we weren't going to go far without a prop. What to do? While I had always preached that most troller fishermen were excellent problem solvers, this was clearly one situation that called for some sort of divine intervention. Probably the only place in the whole of Canada where one would have a chance of finding a suitable replacement propeller on no notice of any kind was Ed Pallister's junk yard in Sooke, BC.

The reader must appreciate that this was not a problem with a simple solution. When a boat is fitted out, the propeller is usually a stock item ordered months in advance. However, the propeller has to be machined on a lathe to create the appropriate bore and taper to fit the drive shaft from the engine. This is a custom job where measurements are arrived at in microns and days if not weeks are required to fabricate the arrangement. It was a tall order to find an existing propeller that would fit. Taper was not the only problem. We also needed to find a propeller with the correct key way, diameter, pitch and rotation. It was akin to looking for a needle in a haystack.

I arrived at Pallister's Sooke junkyard at about 4 A.M. having driven down the island from the Beachcomber ramp in two hours. I knocked on the door and awakened Ed and informed him of our plight. As always Ed was sympathetic and willing to help. I will always remember Ed's Tennessee drawl. "Oh yeah! If ya go over to that thar other building and work yer way thru them thar aisles up to the third floor and take a look, I think yer might find one."

Working my way through the "aisles" involved going sideways and sucking in my gut to work my way along, all the while screwing in the overhead light bulbs as I made my way to the stairs. I was totally aware that the building was literally groaning under the sheer weight of its contents. Upon arriving at the third floor, I saw a jumble of hundreds upon hundreds of propellers of all shapes and sizes spread out on the floor before me. After spending about three hours crawling around, checking and measuring anything that looked like a possible candidate, to my great relief I found a propeller that would fit.

Again, squeezing down between the aisles, I turned each light off by unscrewing the bulb as I retreated out of the building, dragging the prop with me, to tell Ed that I had found what I needed. When I asked Ed how much I owed him he replied, "Sure, sure, the girl will send ya a bill." Usually his bills arrived within a year. [2]

Returning to Beachcomber Marina, the propeller was fitted to *Marine Link #I* and we backed off the ramp on the next tide.

2. Unfortunately, no one ever captured the full story of Ed Pallister of Sooke. He was a one-of-a-kind who died in 2002. Three years later much of Pallister's junk yard burned down.

THE SALVAGE OF THE PACKER CAPE CALVERT

Tim and I were always alert to any money-making opportunity that came into our line of vision. I recall an event in 1978, the year we first used the *ML#1* in the roe herring fishery. The *Cape Calvert,* a BC Packers vessel, with a full load of fifty tons of herring in her hold, ran aground on rocks near Nanoose Bay, to the north of Nanaimo. It was not long before the vessel, helped by a flooded hold, slipped off the rocks into deeper water where she became fully submerged at a depth of 150 feet (46 m).

Ray Lund, the insurer's representative and marine surveyor, offered us a contract to assist in the salvage operation, initially as the diver/tender vessel. We positioned the *ML#I* over the wreck and divers entered and exited the water over the lowered bow ramp. In the salvage process, the divers first affixed inflatable air bags to the vessel as flotation devices. The *Cape Calvert* was lifted off the bottom in two stages, rerigging the air bags until the vessel was partially above water. The *ML#I* then towed the hulk into Nanoose Bay a short distance away and up onto a mudbank at the south end of the bay. Before a temporary patch could be fitted to the

The BC Packers herring packer *Cape Calvert* is seen here on a mudflat at Nanoose Bay, along with the *ML#I*. Note the inflated flotation bags hanging on the vessel which were used in the salvage to raise the boat. (circa 1978)

damaged vessel, the rotting herring had to be removed from the boat's hold. Tim and I were then awarded a follow-on contract to remove all the diesel fuel and other liquids from the vessel as well as the rapidly putrefying herring. The diesel fuel had long since leaked out and dissipated and there was none remaining.

That left the rotten herring. Rotting fish always smells bad enough, but a full load of some fifty tons stinks to high heaven. Apart from the smell, caused by sour methane gas given off in the rotting process, contact with the skin or clothing quickly permeates both, so a person smells like the worst sort of "walking garbage dump." Merely to be in the presence of a person who reeked of this stuff was sufficient to transfer some of the odour to oneself.

Tim's practicality now came to the fore and we were in our glory trying to figure out how best to remove the mess. We rented the largest portable air compressor we could find and rolled it onto the *ML#I* across the Schooner Cove boat ramp. This along with a 10' length of 8" pvc water pipe were the components of a water/air-lift system. A circular hole was cut in the pipe about a foot up from one end and then the air line from the compressor was inserted through the hole. This formed an air/water column in the pipe that acted much like a super "wet" vacuum cleaner. The air compressor cranked up to the max and the right amount of water mixed in with the herring resulted in a great geyser of "mush" that shot from the pipe into the air 10' high and landed everywhere. We didn't care so long as the

Ray Sauriol, owner of K&K Kustom Metal in Victoria, one of the contractors we could always rely on. Ray and his crew did all the aluminum welding and refurbishing on the *ML#I*.

mess was out of the boat. We completed this operation through two night shifts and the seagulls and crabs cleaned up all the evidence during the day-light high tide.

Mission accomplished we made our way to a local pub, the Arlington Inn, for a well-earned beer and a meal. Unbeknownst to us, we were giving off such powerful fumes that the management seated us at the far end of the kitchen for our meal to avoid the inevitable complaints from the other patrons. The Arlington Inn still stands by the highway near the junction with Northwest Bay Road, just south of Parksville. Still smelling like a garbage dump, Tim and I were treated like lepers by everybody until the sour methane gas had been washed clean from our bodies and clothes—some six or seven days later. We discovered that no amount of showering or washing could alter this time frame.

The salvage of the *Cape Calvert* opened our eyes for new opportunities and Marine Link Transportation has since been involved in numerous boat and plane salvage jobs.

Herring being unloaded from skiffs into the hold of the *SSI#I*. The red and yellow squares are the official flag colours of Seafood Products Ltd.

Tug *Joe Drinkwater* is towing the barge *SSI#I* during herring packing operations. (circa 1982)

Tug *Joe Drinkwater* is again towing the barge *SSI#I* with the *ML#I* tied alongside on the left. Note the "CASH" sign on the barge *(see p.21)* and the bridle set up on the towline.

Chapter 3

WHEN PEOPLE GO CRAZY

When I look back some forty years to that time in my life when I was heavily involved in the seasonal roe herring fishery, I realize the madness of it all. Many times I have asked myself, "How did we get away with it?" Who in their right mind would hang out a 4' x 8' sign advertising "CASH" on board?

That is exactly what we did. In 1979 the price of herring bought on the fishing grounds reached the astronomical level of $5,000 per ton, sometimes more. It was not uncommon for some seine boats to make $200,000 on a single set with some of the bigger boats taking catches ranging close to the million dollar mark. Gillnet fishermen at the right spot, operating a two- or three-man herring skiff, could earn $50,000 for a night's shaking of their nets. These nets were set close in and parallel to the shore as herring moved into the shallow water to spawn.

In the 1979 fishery things got truly out of hand. From 1977–1980 a value bubble[1] had developed where herring roe prices out on the fishing grounds were so bizarre that any far thinker knew it would end badly. But if one wanted to be in the game, the main requirement was to have cash. In March 1979 I found myself carrying $750,000 cash on my person. The two bundles of freshly minted $1,000 bills[2] were in one money belt around my midriff and two other belts held bundles of $100 bills. My briefcase was filled with $50 bills and additional $100 bills. I also had a strong box full of tens, twenties and fifties. Our operation for SSI Sea Products was small compared to some other buyers on the grounds who at times carried more than a million dollars cash.

It was simply crazy! Many times when the fishing was good our crew, now ten, would work around the clock, while I handled the paperwork. Again, picture me at 2 A.M., completely exhausted, running on empty, counting out $20,000 or $30,000 dollars in cash for receipt of six tons of herring. After a while we felt we were just part of a giant Monopoly game—only we played with real money. We worked on a commission basis which meant "no fish no pay." Sometimes we handed a fisherman $1,000 in cash for a measly 300 lb. (136 kg) of herring.

The 1980 roe herring fishery proved to

1. The bubble burst after 1981 and the price paid to the fishermen has steadily declined, to $300 per ton in the roe herring fishery just concluded, 2015.
2. $1,000 bills were discontinued by the Canadian mint around 1990.

be the peak and the value bubble did indeed burst. It was a complete blowout for us. Three of the team had gone AWOL and who could blame them? When the price went above $4,500 dollars per ton, SSI called us home and paid us wages for our time, although John Christenson and Ken Olding were under no obligation to do so under our commission/buyer status. SSI Sea Products Ltd. never went back into the fishery and sold the *SSI#I* barge to Lee Roberts of Quadra Island.

LEE ROBERTS

Lee Roberts has a long history with Marine Link Transportation (MLT) and Campbell River Marine Terminal (CRMT). When Lee bought the *SSI#I* he turned it into a pile-driving platform, which later built much of our new terminal at Menzies Bay. More on this later. I took my herring packing operation to Seafood Products Ltd. in Port Hardy where I knew the principal owner, Don Cruikshank, during my time in the salmon fishery. Seafood Products had processing plants at Port Hardy and Vancouver Harbour. Lee, with his tugboat the *Joe Drinkwater,* and the barge *SSI#I,* teamed up with Marine Link and *ML#I*, our landing craft, for the next eight roe herring seasons.

In retrospect, the 1979 and 1980 roe herring fisheries were nothing short of a maritime gold rush. Those few who recognized it as such prospered, knowing it would not last. Others were less wise and unprepared when the value bubble burst and the tax man came knocking.

Today, the roe herring fishery is reduced considerably. The cash element has gone from the scene entirely and now all deliveries of roe herring are "booked" for later settlement. We were extremely vulnerable when we advertised ourselves as "cash buyers," but to my knowledge no one was ever robbed. However, I did hear rumours that one or two packer/buyers had absconded with the cash.

THE RCMP BECOME INVOLVED

The cash frenzy evident in the roe herring fishery between 1978 and 1980 did not go unnoticed by the RCMP. In 1979 Tim and I were interviewed by officers of the Parksville detachment and the RCMP Marine Division. We exchanged important contact information and they gave us a briefing on the do's and don'ts of handling cash out on the fishing grounds. One of their main points was to be observant of anything that did not belong and looked "out of place" We were asked to record the serial numbers of at least a third of the cash bills in our possession, partricularly the older bills in the bundles received from the bank which had no serial number sequence. Our pictures were taken, apparently for ease of identification. We were asked to bring in whatever cash bills we could in advance of the fishery opening and these were invisibly marked and returned to us. All in all it was a fascinating education for both of us.

Lee Roberts operating his pile-driving crane on board the *SSI#I.*

THE BARGE SSI#1

The *Saltspring Island #I* (*SSI#I)* was a flat-bottomed barge about 90' in length and 30' in beam. It was constructed of ferro-concrete, which is a proven type of vessel construction first pioneered in France in the late eighteenth century. Some sizeable ships were constructed of ferro-concrete in WWI in the UK and the US. Recently, a number of fishboats in BC have been of ferro-concrete construction. Essentially, it is a process of forming a thick cage of steel rebar and heavy wire mesh into the shape and lines of a hull. The shaped hull is then impregnated with concrete to about a 1 1/2" to 2" thickness, hopefully in one continuous concrete pour and insuring that all rebar and wire are completely sealed and no air pockets are left in the concrete. The main advantages of ferro-concrete are its relatively lower cost of maintenance and construction and the fact that it is impervious to attack from teredos and other marine organisms, as well as rust and rot.

The *SSI#I* had three large holds, each capable of holding about fifty tons of herring. Each end of the barge had a foam-filled compartment running back about 15' which formed sealed watertight compartments. This ensured the barge would have positive flotation and freeboard, even with the three holds fully flooded. The tanks each had a flush deck hatch of about 5' by 6' dimensions which were covered by thick planks set into a combing when not in use. The builder of the *SSI#I* is unknown but John Christenson acquired it sometime before 1974.

YOU GET THAT SINKING FEELING: A STORY FROM THE 1982 HERRING FISHERY

During the 1982 roe herring fishery we continued to engage Lee Roberts and his tug the *Joe Drinkwater,* towing the barge *SSI#I.*

Lee had built a two-storey housework on the stern of the barge which served as extra living accommodation and supply storage for the host of fittings and gear he needed for his pile-driving and wharf construction business. This housework was built over a number of large winches for the anchoring system which was used while engaged in piledriving. Each time the barge was involved in herring packing, the actual pile-driving crane was removed.

When the three below-deck holds of the *SSI#I* were fully loaded with 150 tons of herring, the barge had minimal freeboard. We usually trimmed the barge such that the stern had about 12" of freeboard, while the bow had about 18". As long as good weather prevailed, there was no problem during the ten-hour tow to Vancouver Harbour and the Seafood Products plant. Nevertheless, with the freeboard described, we needed to be very careful about sea conditions, most particularly wave height.

Everything went well in the fishery and we got a full load into the *SSI#I* from the area around Denman and Hornby Islands where the spawning had been particularly heavy. We headed for Vancouver Harbour with the *Joe Drinkwater* towing the fully laden barge and the fully loaded *ML#1* tied alongside as an assist boat. Everything went well as we approached Point Atkinson with its prominent lighthouse signalling the approaches to Vancouver Harbour. It was about 4 A.M. with flat calm conditions. We could see the lights of the city and make out the Lions Gate bridge ahead when fate

The barge *SSI#I* is fully loaded with 150 tons of herring, ready for towing to the Seafood Products Ltd. processing plant in Vancouver Harbour. Note the housework at the stern of the barge.

intervened. The ebb tide out of Burrard Inlet (Vancouver Harbour) had created nasty sea conditions and large steep waves had built up. This condition was known to fishermen as "tide lump" and the waves suddenly enveloped the barge as we crossed from quiet water into the ebb tidal current. The *SSI#I* began taking on water and she started to sink. With the stern beginning to settle deeper in the water, objects on the deck of the barge were floating off. We knew we were in trouble.

With the *ML#I* lashed alongside and pushing hard, Lee went to full power in the tug. As mentioned earlier, the *SS1#1* had built-in flotation in the stern and bow sections which were sealed and watertight, but Lee had added additional weight with the installation of the housework and winches for his pile-driving operation. This made for a difference in flotation and now the barge was sinking by the stern. As long as we kept her moving the flooding was reduced and the rate of sinking was stabilized. A third of the barge was still under the water and we needed to keep the pumps at full power. We were already in the

AL'S "LIGHTS OUT SPECIAL"

No fish bought meant no earnings. Competition between cash buyers on the fishing grounds was very aggressive and the fishermen enjoyed a super-heated "seller's market."

To secure product we needed to be "competitive." There are more ways to be competitive than simply the amount of services rendered or dollars paid. These two elements are indeed important but one might use other means to sharpen your competitive position. As an example, out on the roe herring grounds there were a number of buyers, one of the largest being the Prince Rupert Fishermen's Co-operative. Co-op members were prominent in the roe herring fishery and they were obliged to unload their catch to Co-op packers. However, the Co-op packer vessels were not "cash buyers" and had no cash on board except for very minor advances for groceries, outboard motor fuel, etc. Deliveries of fish to Co-op packers were "booked" for later settlement and payout to Co-op members.

If one was smart one could exploit these circumstances and I did. Co-op fishermen would cruise by the *ML#I* or the *SSI#I* barge in the daylight hours and ask me how much I was paying. I would respond with the number and then make sure they understood that there was what I called "lights out special" every night between midnight and 2 A.M. Occasionally a Co-op skiff full of herring would loom out of the darkness as our deck illumination lights had been turned out for this two-hour period each night. We would unload the skiff and read the scale by flashlight, do the paper work by flashlight and count the money by flashlight, and no one would be any the wiser. The Co-op fishermen would depart with cash in their pockets. This also worked occasionally to secure a skiff-load of fish from non-Co-op fishermen as well.

The *SSI#I* with tugboat *Joe Drinkwater* alongside. The crane was removed for herring packing.

approaches to the Lions Gate Bridge and we all knew that if the barge, with its full load of herring, sank under the bridge in the First Narrows we would be very unpopular, to say the least. We imagined a scenario before us of herring washing up on every beach and in the harbour itself for miles around, not to mention the fallout if the barge sank and became a navigational hazard.

Lee was the man of the moment, calm and clear thinking. We were close in shore to West Vancouver where Lee knew there was a Department of Fisheries and Oceans (DFO) piling dock. We prayed that it was still there and free of other boats and that we could reach it before the barge sank beyond the point of recovery. We made it, to our great relief, tied up to the wharf and got all pumps working at full bore.

The commissionaire on security patrol at the wharf came down to find out what was happening and sized up the situation. He asked if there was anything he could do to help, which we appreciated. By now the pumps were gaining and the stern started to come back up. We moved out on the next incoming tide and quickly towed up harbour to the Seafood Products dock. We had escaped disaster by the skin of our teeth—largely due to Lee Roberts.

Marine Link #I fully loaded with tote boxes of roe herring, alongside *SSI#I*. The boom of *ML#I* is being used to swing the lifts of herring from a skiff (not shown) across into the chute on the *SSI#I*. Note the large dial-scale in the lifting apparatus.

A herring skiff with a herring gillnet laid out ready to be deployed. When fishing, these nets are pulled across the power roller on the right, with two or three men in each skiff, at the bow and the stern, handling the net.

HONEST SAM SMITH

One man among many who stands out in my memory is Sam Smith, a truly unique individual who, along with his brother Rennie Smith, became known as the elder statesmen of the West Coast of Vancouver Island troll salmon fishery. They both had a heavy attachment to the coastal village of Kyuquot and both were "highliner" fishermen who started in the industry back in the 1940s. These were the guys who could tell you about the cyclical nature of the salmon resource and both, Sam in particular, were very shrewd businessmen in their own right. When the time came for me to find a new accountant, colleagues pointed me to Sam and Rennie Smith for their advice.

Sam was well into his seventies when I came to know him as a solid advisor during my watch as President of the Pacific Trollers Association, 1982–1984. In those days, the troll salmon season ran from April 15th to the end of October, that is if you wanted to fish that hard. Sam also had a skiff and a roe herring licence and participated in the roe herring gillnet fishery each year in the Strait of Georgia. Sam made a number of sizeable deliveries to our barge during the 1982 fishery. I tabulated the brailed lifts and then counted out cash to Sam as was the standard drill. The money was counted and recounted until we were nearly blind.

A month later, after the fishery was over, I received a phone call from Sam, enquiring whether or not I had reconciled my cash account and did it balance? Was I out $100? He explained that he had taken $50,000 cash to deposit at his bank and when the teller counted the money, with that special flick of the thumb that tellers have,[3] she had separated two $100 bills stuck together. This being the case I had overpaid him and he was returning the $100. I couldn't bring myself to tell Sam that I had balanced to within $1,000, which was considered a good outcome. Returning the $100 overpayment was, I thought, a true measure of the man—which we seldom see today.

3. Cash counting machines did not exist at that time.

Chapter 4

THE FREIGHT BUSINESS

We soon found that the lengthened *Marine Link #I* opened up new possibilities for us as potential customers enquired about our capability to transport other forms of cargo. Tim took over the operation of the *ML#I,* initially based at Sidney, BC, but the volume of freight obtainable in that location amounted to only two days' work a week.

The seasonal roe herring fishery gave work for the boat in February and March of each year, but it left *ML#I* looking for work wherever it could be obtained in the off-season months from April through to the following February.

We decided to move further north. Tim moved his live-aboard boat *Three Sons III*

ML#I, now lengthened to 54', in Gorge Harbour on Cortes Island. (circa 1980)

Judy and Tim Campbell with son Marty on their live-aboard fishboat *Three Sons III.* (circa 1979)

and his family to Cortes Island where a new base of operation was set up. Cortes Island was somewhat off the beaten track, but for available work it was a big improvement. Carol Guthrie, a long-time resident of the island, was hired to provide an answering service for Marine Link Transportation and Tim checked with her twice daily.

Soon after settling in at Cortes, Tim and I rethought our strategy and decided to move Marine Link Transportation to Tyee Spit[1] in Campbell River on Vancouver Island. This reduced our need to round Cape Mudge at the southern tip of Quadra Island, which can be quite treacherous in bad weather. Being located in Campbell River definitely made more sense. Campbell River had become the industrial hub for the northern half of Vancouver Island as well as the cluster of islands and mainland inlets opposite. It was also the base for many industrial supply companies which serviced the logging sector. One acre of rented land on Tyee Spit became our base of operations and freight yard.

John Braaten, manager of the Whonnock Industries logging camp in Kingcome Inlet, engaged MLT for a scheduled biweekly run to supply the camp. It was our first significant freight customer. Our job was to take in freight of every description to resupply this year-round logging camp. The operation at Whonnock (later Interfor) involved over a hundred people. It required huge amounts of groceries (refrigerated and frozen), welding supplies, machinery parts, dry goods, steel, laundry, tires, oxyacetelene gas, explosives for road building and much more. The camp was located 2 km (1.2 mi) up the Kingcome River from its mouth. The previous carrier,

1. Tyee Spit is a typical spit of land formed by freshet high water flows that deposit sandy sediment at the river mouth. These deposits build up over time and help define the estuary of the river. The same dynamic can take place in certain areas of heavy tidal flow. Examples are Sidney Spit, an extension of Sidney Island, and Whiffen Spit, at the entrance to Sooke Harbour.

A pickup receiving groceries from *ML#I* at the Whonnock Industries camp in Kingcome Inlet.

Another view of unloading freight at Kingcome Inlet.

Al Meadows is on the right of *ML#I's* wheelhouse operating the hydraulic boom while unloading freezer goods at Kingcome Inlet.

A specialized container for groceries off-loading at Kingcome Inlet.

Marine Link warehouse on Tyee Spit. This is the building that threatened to blow away in high winds. Note our first forklift in the foreground.

Warehouseman Vic Wedel seen here surrounded by groceries ready for loading and transport to a logging camp.

Coast Ferries, deposited all the freight on a huge float at tidewater. Whonnock crews were then taken off their regular logging activity and spent days moving these supplies, with considerable loss and additional cost. It had become unworkable for the company. Marine Link was able to deliver all these materials directly up the river on the *ML#1* and off-load right at the camp. This was a much more desirable scenario and it worked well for all parties concerned.

These land-based, stand-alone, year-round logging camps are now a thing of the past. The Bendickson camp at Fraser Bay at the head of Loughborough Inlet is one of the last survivors.

This opportunity to service Whonnock in Kingcome Inlet was the springboard for MLT to become recognized as a significant player in the coastal freight and barging business. Marine Link Transportation's first base of operation was the Rosmar freight yard on Tyee Spit and it continued there for sixteen years, 1980–1996.

ML#1 loading general freight at Tyee Spit yard. Helper Barry Haas is operating a Bull Moose forklift.

A view of *ML#I* loading at Tyee Spit. An example of "hotloading" where the freight comes directly from the truck onto the boat.

Our first employees, Vic Wedel *(l)* and Gunnar Brostrom, showing their innovative skills while unloading a small bulldozer at Tyee Spit using two forklifts.

ML#I at Redonda Bay, West Redonda Island. Al is the man hooking up the lift as he unloads heavy cable to a logging operation. It was a one-person crew, as was usual with *ML#I*.

Our first office at Tyee Spit.

As early as the 1960s Campbell River was considered the float plane capital of Canada. Half a dozen float plane operators were based out of Tyee Spit, as well as a couple of helicopter operations. However, this proximity to aircraft taking off and landing proved to be a problem for our operation, especially during poor weather conditions and high winds sweeping across the low-lying spit. A tidal bar added further complications as the vessels coming and going were tidal bound requiring high water to cross this bar.

In the beginning, the loading operation at Tyee Spit was what is termed "hotloading." This takes place where the truck delivering the freight to the yard actually meets the boat and the freight is then lifted directly onto the deck of *ML#1*. When we bought our first forklift to assist moving the freight around the yard, we thought we had died and gone to heaven. This forklift is an 8,000 lb (3,628.7 kg), dual-wheel Lansing Bagnell machine purchased second hand from BC Conveying Machinery in 1982. We still use this forklift today.

Tim and I rented a sixteen-foot worn-out travel trailer from a commercial fishing colleague, Art Cheshire, and this became our first "office" at Tyee Spit. *(see p.34)* The contents were one telephone, a small table, a heater, a bunk bed and, depending on the time of year, either two inches of dust or mud, but it was functional—and the phone did ring. Many were the nights that Tim or I overnighted in "the office" with the trailer absolutely shaking from the strong wind. The *ML#1* would arrive and be reloaded at 4 AM. And so the business grew.

As the volumes increased and we began moving perishable freight such as groceries for logging camps, we needed a covered warehouse and a washroom. Marine Link was able to rent an old aircraft maintenance hangar from Coval Air, a float plane operator on the spit. I remember well that the wind would lift the roof of this building and many times it was very close to being blown away. Each night we would back the forklift up against the freight door on the southeast exposure just to keep the building intact. In the movement of freight from the warehouse to the bulkhead, our forklift had to cross driveways and dodge all manner of vehicles, the worst of which were taxis in a rush to meet a plane or deposit a passenger. We never had a collision, but it was close many times.

In 1989, we hired our first employees. Gunnar Brostrom was our yardman/forklift operator "on call." Gunnar had been a tree faller previously, but he had had enough of working in the bush and now was the sign installer for Quality Signs in Campbell River, owned and operated by Gunnar's wife Marita. We could call upon Gunnar at any time to help out in our freight yard. We also hired Vic Wedel as a full-time yardman. Previously he had worked at Whitecrest Mills until that operation folded. Vic is still with us today, the senior yardman at CRMT.

A view of the Marine Link Tyee Spit freight yard. Note the office on the right-hand side.

ML#I at its Tyee Spit base with a very unique freight item. The object on deck is a fibreglass cone removed by helicopter from a mountain top in Toba Inlet. The cone was used to house and protect a relay station for communication apparatus. This cargo was loaded into the *ML#I* and unloaded by helicopter.

STABILITY OF A SHIP

A captain in charge of a ship, from the largest to the smallest, should have stability as a primary concern. It is possibly the most important factor in maintaining the safety of the ship and all aboard. We read of vessels capsizing after being overloaded with passengers or freight, with inadequate life saving apparatus or crew training, leading to significant loss of life. We most often hear of these tragedies happening in the Phillipines, Indonesia, Bangladesh, Greece, Italy and other countries. In Canada, Transport Canada Ship Safety Division is the responsible government agency and it does a good job. In spite of this, occasionally accidents do happen in our own backyard, like the sinking of the *Queen of the North* and the *Sundancer.* *(see p.86)*

"Transport Canada-certified vessel crew" means that vessels such as the *Aurora Explorer* meet these reguatory requirements. All commercial vessels over fifteen gross tons are inspected by the Ship Safety Division and the *Aurora Explorer,* in particular, has superior stability characteristics due to its barge-type hull configuration.

LIVING IN A TELEPHONE BOOTH

The cabin in the *Marine Link #I* contained a small bunk. From the deckhead, a sizeable chart table hinged down over this bunk with a small diesel stove opposite. The helm control panel, alarm panel, radar, searchlight handles, autopilot and various gauges and switches completed the array of controls in front of the helmsman's chair. It was tight but comfortable and only measuring 5' X 6', slightly larger than the size of a telephone booth.

Cooking on the *ML#I* was an art form that Tim and I developed with precision. Before starting on a trip we purchased "ready-to-eat" meals. A truly effective way to cook a hot meal during any season or any weather was to place the foil package on top of the engine exhaust muffler at the back of the wheelhouse for about ten minutes. An ice-chest cooler secured on the back deck rounded out the galley.

Usually, trips were undertaken with a one-man crew. When we had freight for R&N Logging, at Hayden Bay in Loughborough Inlet, we would manoeuvre things so the boat arrived at night and therefore we would get "invited for breakfast" in camp. Fred Koch was a great supporter of Marine Link and was very generous in driving down to the camp dock before the first rays of daylight to take Tim or me to breakfast. Fred was another friend who made a major contribution to the success of Marine Link Transportation.

A FLOATING MONEY TREE

Any homeowner who has a Western red cedar shake or shingle roof knows how costly that type of roof is. Large red cedar trees are only found in southern coastal BC forests. *(see p.139)* In the early 1900s the logging industry technology was the axe and the two-man crosscut handsaw. Logs were skidded out of the forest using teams of oxen or a steam donkey. *(see p.145)* The easily accessible first-growth fir and spruce were "high-graded" while stands of hemlock were avoided.[2] Red cedar had no market and therefore no value. It was considered a "weed tree" as was alder, another abundant coastal species until the 1990s. Huge red cedar trees were often felled and left on the forest floor to rot. Eventually, the forest cover regenerated and these giant cedar logs disappeared into the landscape of moss and other organic material from the surrounding ecosphere.

Western red cedar takes a very long time to rot and that, along with its highly decorative finish and clear grain, are why it is so widely sought after for roofing and decorative siding. Finding and salvaging felled first-growth cedar logs has been a major acitivity since the 1960s and continues to the present. Typically, these giants are found in excellent condition once the thin surface deterioration is cleared away. Salvage cedar is cut by chainsaw into "blocks" of specific lengths (18"-24") and lifted by helicopter out of the forest utilizing a cargo net to a nearby landing and assembly area. The value of cedar blocks is high, usually sufficiently high as to warrant these high extraction costs.[3] These blocks would then go to a mill where they were processed into shakes or shingles.

This brief history is the backdrop to an unusal event that Tim and the *ML#I* participated in around 1992. A barge load of cedar blocks under tow through Gillard Pass, the channel between Sonora and Stuart Islands near the mouth of Bute Inlet, spilled off the barge. The tug boat captain had miscalculated the slack water timing for the Yuclata Rapids, which are a navigational hazard of the pass. The out-of-control barge in the swirling riptides and whirlpools of the rapids had heeled over and jettisoned its load into the water. Cedar blocks were spread over miles of coastline.

This resulted in a mad scramble by all and sundry local boats to recover these floating "gold nuggets." The *ML#I* was ideally suited for the purpose with the bow ramp lowered to just above the water line. Deckhands Jussi Nahri and Brent Adams (Guy Adams' brother), each armed with a pike pole, hoisted the blocks aboard as Tim piloted the boat slowly through the sea of cedar blocks. The recovery took weeks and Tim remembers selling several loads back to the insurance company who covered the loss. Who says there's no money tree? In this case a floating one.

2. Hemlock is the predominant softwood species in BC coastal forests.
3. The cedar shake block market varies greatly, but cedar generally holds its value better than other coastal forest species.

(left) ML#I. Tim is on the right at the hydraulic boom control. He is loading building supplies for transport back to Campbell River.

(below) ML#I with a full load of lumber and a "bone in its teeth," a large bow wave. Seen in Bute Inlet.

SERVICING THE SALMON FARMING INDUSTRY

The salmon farming industry was introduced to the coastal waters of BC in the mid-1980s. Salmon farming was a big industry in Norway, Sweden and Scotland; it also had a foothold in the Atlantic Maritime Provinces of Canada. In the 1990s Chile also became a large player in the expansion of the salmon aquaculture industry.

When this new activity first came to BC waters, it was concentrated in the Sechelt and Sunshine Coast area, which over the next decade proved to be a less-than-ideal location. Heavy losses from algae bloom, high water temperatures and predation by seals and sea lions resulted in most of the fish farms relocating to Johnstone and Queen Charlotte Straits. Some farms relocated to the west coast of Vancouver Island and to a lesser extent around Prince Rupert and the Central BC Coast.

Much controversy has dogged this new industry such that today all growth and expansion is going to Chile. Marine Link had the opportunity to service fish farms in the Campbell River and Johnstone Strait areas, mainly due to Whitecrest Mills (a manufacturer of fish food) initially setting up operations in the industrial park just north of Campbell River. During the late 1980s and early 1990s, the *ML#1* was often employed on a round-the-clock basis, delivering fish food supplies to the farms. Eventually, Whitecrest Mills went out of business as it could not compete with the much larger fish food manufacturers located in the Vancouver area on the lower Fraser River. Marine Link's servicing of the aquaculture industry has waned since the 1990s.

Most people do not realize that upwards of 80 percent of "seafood" consumed world wide comes from fish-farming aquaculture, or mariculture which pertains to shellfish. While wild stocks of fish have generally been maintained at sustainable levels off North America's Pacific Coast, this is not the case in the other oceans of the world. Aquaculture in BC waters mainly involves the production of Atlantic salmon which are not indigenous to the Pacific Ocean. However, reasonable improvement in operations and applications are taking place in the industry. An example of this is engineered anchoring systems that provide better security over previous systems where the pen assembly anchors were nothing more than large ten- or twenty-ton concrete blocks, with a rope attached, dropped in deep water.

In my opinion, salmon farming in BC waters is headed down the same path that logging took from the 1920s to the present day. The improvements in road building, including road deactivation after harvesting, silviculture technology and resource extraction processes are now leading edge techniques that provide for a much-improved sustainability of the timber resource.

Aquaculture in BC will likely develop the same way logging has. Over the last twenty years it has demonstrated the ability to move forward with sound environmental practices.

A TRIP TO REMEMBER

During the offseason from fishing, I became increasingly involved in running the *Marine Link #1* and giving Tim some time off. A memorable trip was in the winter of 1983 when I ran *ML#1* up to the head of Knight Inlet to deliver a much-needed generator set to a DFO crew working at a hatchery project on the Klinaklina River. Knight is the longest mainland inlet on the southern half of the BC coast and takes one from the warmer maritime climate of the coast into the interior climate of severe cold.

In doing this trip it was clear that I would likely face winter outflow winds of up to 145 km (90 mi) per hour, which are a common feature when entrenched high pressure in the interior of BC creates high winds and plunging temperatures coming down the mainland inlets. This tests the ship and, in this case, the small crew of one, for I had no company on this trip. Life on board was spartan, but comfortable, with ready-to-eat meals and limited facilities.

From the moment I left Campbell River weather conditions were questionable and I knew I would be encountering the boat icing up from the salt water spray over the bow and the wind chill hovering around -30ºC. In any situation where a vessel encounters icing, there is a question of the boat maintaining stability. Too much ice forming on the upper superstructure and hull of a ship is very dangerous and if it is not removed it severely compromises the stability, such that the ship might capsize. Fortunately, this is not a major concern for landing craft-type vessels. Much of the ice ends up down low in the cargo well deck and in effect becomes additional cargo. This effectively lowers the centre of gravity and preserves the seaworthiness of the vessel. The severe winter conditions meant that I dare not turn the engine off for fear of not getting it started again; indeed, the warmth from the truck heater[4] mounted on the floor of the wheelhouse was needed to heat the cabin.

I had cobbled together a 5' length of 3" hose which I clamped onto the truck heater. With the heater fan running, hot air was played onto the wheelhouse windows looking forward over the bow. This melted the ice buildup on the window and provided limited vision ahead.

After departing Campbell River, I managed to clear Johnstone Strait and on the third day by nightfall I was about a third of the way up Knight Inlet where I tied up to a logging camp barge at Sally Creek. Fortunately, the logging crew had gone home as a result of the cold and snow. Only a watchman was left in camp.

After waiting two days for the wind to go down and the weather to improve, I decided that I could wait no longer. I let go from the camp barge at first light the next morning. My plan was to jog my way up the inlet at low speed, hugging the shore line and seeking lee from the wind and seas wherever I could find it, hoping to arrive by nightfall. As I approached the head of the inlet I encountered heavy skim ice about an inch thick that had formed on the surface due to fresh outflow water emptying into

4. A truck heater receives hot water coming off the engine's fresh water cooling jacket which passes through coils in the heater and a fan blows heat off the coils and into whatever compartment the heater is located. This works very efficiently and can heat up a space very quickly.

the inlet from the Klinaklina and Franklin Rivers and neighbouring creeks. Care and attention must be exercised by the operator of a vessel breaking a pathway through ice. Even a metal hull can be punctured very easily, with disastrous consequences.

I eased *ML#1* into the ice and got to within sight of the landing, about two miles away, before the ice became too thick and I was stuck, hard and fast. Darkness was coming so I heated up a ready-to-eat meal on the engine exhaust, left the engine idling (it had not been shut down for five days) and put my head down for the night.

Morning brought a welcome change in wind direction and speed with some moderation in air temperature, all of which allowed me to get the boat to the landing. My delivery to the DFO crew amounted to one large ice cube, at the centre of which was a large box containing the new generator. The crew had been waiting anxiously as all their other generator sets had failed. I quickly got a signature for delivery and it was time to get down the inlet. I made record time with a following wind and sea back into Johnstone Strait. When I got back to our base at Tyee Spit in Campbell River the *ML#1* was still covered with four inches of ice.

Bill Forte and partner Gwen. Bill was always a great supporter of Marine Link and was the pioneer in freight transport in Johnstone Strait with his powered barge the *Inlet Vagabond.*

Chapter 5

AT A CROSSROADS: A NEW BUILDING PROJECT

On several occasions, Fred Koch of R&N Logging had told us that Marine Link needed a larger boat, and that old tenet "you either grow or die in business" weighed heavily. I knew I had to make a decision. I had been working actively to relieve Tim during the salmon fishing off-season and I also realized that soon I would have to choose between commercial fishing and growing out Marine Link Transportation.

Financing for a larger boat was the critical element. If I sold the *Lyra* I would have at least seed money. So far as fishing was concerned, the writing had been on the wall for some time. The West Coast of Vancouver Island troll salmon fishery was front and centre and disputes with the Americans over Canadian interception of their salmon stocks heading for Washington and Oregon rivers and the Alaskan interceptions of BC-bound salmon were generally settled in favour of the Americans. I was tired of the ever-increasing politics that had invaded the fishing industry.

I was also tired of painting the same board year after year in keeping the *Lyra* in shape. On top of the annual routine, I had taken on various board-of-director positions, including a two-year stint as president of the Pacific Trollers Association. Under my watch the membership of this organization had grown to its highest ever with 550 dues-paying owner/operator members organized in twelve different branches along the BC Coast. I was also a regular columnist for *Western Fisheries* magazine, a popular but now-defunct trade journal for the BC fishing industry.

By 1986 I had reached a crossroads. At thirty-five years of age I made my decision, sold the *Lyra* and exited the commercial fishing industry. The money I realized from the sale of my boat I hoped would provide enough equity to leverage sufficient financing for a new build. I again engaged the services of Ron Thicke, naval architect, and together we collaborated on the design of what was to become the *Marine Link #II*. Of course, the biggest challenge Tim and I faced was how to finance the new build. Many meetings were held with the chartered bank that I had financed the *Lyra* through. My credit was excellent but we still went through many hoops with the bank. At the end, the bank proved to be uninterested in funding our expansion.

It was also important to have a business accountant that one could rely on for sound advice and timely processing of company records and tax issues. Initially, we used the services of a large well-known national firm, but it soon became apparent that they were treating their professional obligations to MLT as low priority. Revenue Canada was getting on our case and the national firm was making excuses. I sought advice from a number of personal mentors and fishing colleagues. I wanted a chartered accountant who would think outside the box and the name that came up frequently was Mike Pinch, who had an office out in Brentwood Bay on the Saanich Peninsula. I approached Mike and thus began, and continues to this day, not only a professional business relationship but a personal friendship. Pinch and Associates have been MLT's accountant for thirty years and lately CRMT, which speaks for itself.

For a number of months I researched alternatives for financing the *ML#II* but came up empty. It was truly a watershed moment when Fred Koch sought me out in our freight yard in September 1987 and handed me a business card for one John Hitchcock, president and CEO of Forest & Marine Financial Corporation (F&M) in Nanaimo. I remember vividly Fred's comments to me at the time when he said, "I have never had a good night's sleep with a chartered bank, but I get a very good night's sleep with these people. I am going to 'kick your ass' if you don't go and see John Hitchcock."

I took Fred's advice and met John in his office in Nanaimo four days later and we reviewed the plans for the new vessel. Unlike the bank, John asked intelligent questions. We had a very good meeting. Two days later I received approval for a $550,000 loan from F&M, all on a handshake, a personal guarantee which was removed once the vessel was completed and launched and replaced by a marine mortgage on the boat—total fees $50. Mike Pinch, who I had just hired as the company accountant, was along with me when the paperwork was done for the loan. To the question presented to John, "What kind of reporting do you require during the draw-down of the loan?" came the reply, "Send us a picture from time to time." To this day Mike cannot believe that kind of accommodation was possible from a financier, considering the size of the loan.

It was such a refreshing process after the runaround we had suffered with the bank. The next day I went into the bank, which I had dealt with for the previous seventeen years without a hiccup, and informed them that they were "fired" and I closed out all my accounts with them. It was a very good day.

Thus began an eighteen-year business relationship with Forest & Marine where it would, over time, finance two other vessels, numerous pieces of rolling equipment and the purchase of land and the building of our new terminal. Tim and I would still be a two-boat band if we had not had this kind of total support from John Hitchcock and Forest & Marine.

MY COMMENTS ON CHARTERED BANKS

After forty years in business it is my opinion that the Tier One Canadian chartered banks are fundamentally uninterested in financing or supporting small business. Yes, they do put out their poster-boy ads extolling support for this or that activity for young people or financing small business somewhere, sometime. But, in my experience, when the rubber meets the road they would rather not. It seems that, generally, the big banks' preference is to expand their presence in Third-World economies such as Costa Rica, Haiti, Equador, Panama, Peru and others, or getting involved in sub-prime mortgages and the ENRONs of this world. My experience has been that the constantly moving goal posts ultimately make it impossible for small business if they are unfortunate enough to have to deal with a Canadian chartered bank. I say this after having been put through the ringer on a number of occasions, either trying to establish a line of credit account or funding a project such as the *ML#II*.

Inevitably, one ends up dealing with a revolving door of junior account loan officers, most of whom are in total "cya" mode. The loan officer may know less about business than you do and are only motivated to follow policy decisions on this or that sector of the economy as determined on Bay Street in far-off Toronto. What the entrepeneur will find is a huge paper burden of reporting and upfront fees that the bank will demand, together with security far in excess of what is necessary. The loan application may carry upfront fees of 2, 3 or 4 percent of the total loan, only some of which will be refundable even if the bank says "no" to the loan. There will be collateral mortgages, personal guarantees, surveys ad nauseum, and much more including legal costs for both sides paid by the borrowing client, all of which amounts to substantial costs before you receive your first dollar of loan funding. This opinion does not extend to the local branch where my businesses have always received excellent co-operation and support by the people behind the counter.

I have had the good fortune of being able to find alternate sources of financing after having been turned down by the bank to build the *ML#II.* There are other sources of financing out there in the business world but one has to work to find them. These include credit unions, venture capitalists, angel financiers, family members and merchant banks such as Forest & Marine Financial Corporation. Also one might consider the second-tier Canadian chartered banks which I believe are more attuned and supportive of small business, but they too can be difficult. The Federal Business Development Bank (FBDB) is also a possibiliity but I would group this particular source of funding with the chartered banks as it can be very costly in terms of reporting and rates charged. When CRMT was about to be built I had struck a deal with the Federal Business Development Bank but ultimately walked away from it for those reasons. Another source of potential financing can be found in share offerings to employees or to family and friends. These are technically difficult and closely regulated by the securities commission and of course the reality is that most employees are risk-adverse. If you have a small business, the Canadian chartered banks and the FBDB should be the lenders of last resort, in my opinion.

CONSTRUCTION OF MARINE LINK #II

Once the vessel plans had been approved by Transport Canada Ship Safety we looked around for a builder. It was an easy decision and Jenkins Marine was awarded the contract to build *Marine Link #II.* It provided considerable flexibility allowing MLT to use our own "in-house" people in the project, alongside the Jenkins workers.

The hull of the *Marine Link #II* was built upside down, given that "downhand welding" was much easier to control. Also, wire-fed automatic welding machines could be used for greater efficiency. The superstructure of *ML#II* was fabricated in aluminum under cover in the Jenkins yard. The third component of the vessel was the bow ramp and John took one look at the design drawings that the naval architect had drawn up and made the comment, "It won't work." We took a leap of faith and accepted John's analysis and left him to find a solution, which he did. With some reworking of the design and the practical input from John, what evolved was a much-improved and fully operable bow ramp that has stood the test of time.

Over the course of the construction, an example of a great work ethic took the form of my nephew, Kevin Brown, who at the age of sixteen helped with various aspects of the construction when he had time away from school. Kevin happily worked in tight, cramped conditions painting virtually every compartment of the vessel. By the time the job was finished, Kevin's coveralls were so stiff with paint they stood up by themselves!

In due course, the hull was turned over and the three components of the vessel, the

John Jenkins *(r)* with company controller Brian Kelly.

My nephew Kevin Brown seen here when he became a third-class engineer with BC Ferries. At age sixteen, he did yeoman service assisting me while we built the *ML#II*.

hull, the aluminum superstructure and the bow ramp, were completed and delivered by truck from the Jenkins yard to the Esquimalt Graving Dock for final assembly. Nickel Bros. house movers handled the move.

During the planning of this operation we were faced with an example of bureaucratic red tape. Our plan was to transport in the early morning one day in May 1988. The route to the dock included the Gorge Road bridge and the Municipality of Esquimalt was worried about the weight of the hull crossing the bridge. The red tape happened when were were told to hire a structural engineer to inspect the bridge and sign off with the municipality that it would not collapse under our weight. I well remember John's comment when he said, "What's the difference between us crossing the bridge with the *ML#II* and several loaded cement trucks crossing the bridge at the same time in traffic?" Would the bridge collapse under the weight of the loaded cement trucks? Not likely. Nevertheless, $800 had to be spent needlessly getting the engineer's stamp of approval before we were permitted to cross the bridge.

CONSTRUCTION OF MARINE LINK #II

The keel plate of *ML#II* laid out in the Jenkins Marine yard on Erskine Lane in Victoria.

Part of the hull is turned over by a large crane after it was welded upside down.

The hull of the *ML#II* starts to come together.

The aluminum superstructure is seen here in a "dry fit" to the hull. It was then lifted off and transported separately to the Esquimalt Graving Dock for final assembly.

The *ML#II* seen here with the bow ramp attached. This was then removed and transported separately to Esquimalt for final fitting to the vessel.

Nickel Bros. heavy transport preparing the hull of *ML#II* for delivery to the Esquimalt Graving Dock. John Jenkins is on the left.

Hilda Meadows christening the new *ML#II.* Note the armouring strips on the hull. These protect the bottom of the vessel when making landings on shore.

The *ML#II* is about to be lifted by the 150-ton railroad crane at the Esquimalt Graving Dock. CFB Esquimalt Naval Base is in the background. (1988)

LAUNCH OF MARINE LINK #II
July 23, 1988

Nickel Bros. did an excellent job of moving the three parts of the *ML#II* from the Jenkins Erskine Road boatyard to the Esquimalt Graving Dock. We successfully crossed the Gorge Road bridge without it collapsing and once the three components were at the dock they were married together and the *ML#II* was complete.

When most ships are launched they slide down a slipway into the water. In the case of *ML#II* it was lifted by the 150-ton railroad crane at the graving dock. Heavy-duty lifting lugs had been welded on the boat, taking many days to complete. We planned a full-fledged launching party. My mother, Hilda, had the honour of breaking the bottle of champagne over the vessel's bow. She was ably assisted by the flower girl, our daughter, Andrea Meadows. With a great fling, Mom hurled the bottle swinging on its rope tether and it simply bounced off. Another try was attempted and it bounced off again. Third time lucky, it smashed over the bow. Invited guests then toured the boat before it was launched. The Jenkins crew had rigged the lifting wire rope slings and engaged the hook on the crane. The boat was swung over the edge of the concrete escarpment and lowered into the briny. A reception followed at Gorge Vale Golf Club, just up the road from the graving dock.

Our new connection with Forest & Marine was working well and we obviously

ML#II in position to be swung over the side of the dock and launched. Note the path of the crane along the railroad tracks.

The *ML#II* being lowered into the briny.

Alan Meadows and Tim Campbell of
Marine Link Transportation Ltd.
Cordially invite you to attend at the launching of their new vessel
"Marine Link II"
July 23, 1988
Launching Ceremony 1:30 pm
Place - Esquimalt Graving Dock,
Admirals Road, Victoria, B.C.
Reception to follow, 2:30-4:30 pm at Gorge Vale Golf Club
1005 Craigflower Road.

Please confirm your attendance to
Dick and Hilda Meadows, 592-9722

had their confidence. However, they were not a full-service bank and we needed to find a local bank for the purposes of a business account, processing deposits and clearing cheques. A full-service bank was needed even if one did not borrow money from them. We chose the Bank of Montreal in Campbell River which we have been with for over twenty-five years.

As completion of the vessel drew near, we found we were short of cash. Cash flow had fallen off as the economy went into a short-term recession which created a credit crunch. The banks were calling loans and fresh financing was just not available as the bankers did what banks usually do in times of crisis. Even Forest & Marine had to take a restrained attitude as one of its main sources of money was a line of credit with a chartered bank, where the bank acted as a wholesaler and F&M was essentially a retailer. *(see p.126)* At this crucial time my father, Dick Meadows, invested $50,000 of direct equity into the company which kept finances on an even keel as the company took delivery of *ML#II*.

TIME WAS RUNNING OUT

I had begun to worry about our tenure at Tyee Spit. The Campbell River waterfront did not offer any viable opportunities regarding a new base of operations. In fact, the handling of many types of freight would be considered dangerous goods and therefore we needed to move as far afield as logistically possible. Part of that decision was an analysis on how far a delivery truck would travel to deliver goods for shipment by barge or vessel without some additional charge. All of this pointed towards Menzies Bay, 15 km (9 mi) north of Campbell River, as the only place having the necessary parameters: available waterfront property, sheltered location from high winds and wave action and yet in close enough proximity for delivery of freight by truck.

A search of ownership confirmed that MacMillan Bloedel Ltd. (MB) owned most of the land fronting Menzies Bay, legally described as District Lot 1 of the Strathcona Regional District. The disposition and management of MB lands was left up to the local divisional offices, which included decisions relating to leaseholds. Later this was changed to a centralized management regime based at the MB headquarters in Vancouver. I approached the Menzies Bay division manager with the proposal of leasing some waterfront land fronting Menzies Bay and found a supportive response. A deal certainly could be struck for our tenancy, but the main problem was MB had a policy that leases were to be a maximum of ten years.

Somehow we had to get around this obstacle. I made the point to them that a ten-year lease would not support over a million dollars of investment and improvements that we would be putting into the leasehold. I whined and complained, and whined and complained some more, such that over the course of several months we finally were offered a twenty-five-year lease. This was unprecedented in MB's history.

Obviously, I had honed my talents of whining to a credible level during my fishing years. This is reminiscent of the "talk, talk, talk persona" that characterized the profession where whining and complaining about "no fish" was the norm. Ultimately the result was very positive for MLT in that we secured six acres of waterfront property in Menzies Bay on a twenty-five-year lease. From that point forward we attempted to find financing to construct our terminal and future base of operation. Financing for improvements on leased property is next to impossible and we had great difficulty. The FBDB offered us a package, but it would have put us in an untenable position very quickly. In my mind, it was far better to leave the land in a raw condition, undeveloped, rather than take on an unworkable financial arrangement.

After five years of being unable to finance and develop our leasehold, our situation was becoming desperate. Every year when we had to cough up the $18,000 lease payment to MB, Tim and I would look at one another and I would say to my partner, "Look at it as a premium on an insurance policy. Sometime in the future we'll be able to make this work." The other difficulty was that the town of Campbell River was anxious to deindustrialize Tyee Spit and we were no longer viewed as a compatible activity. The clock was running out on our tenure there. In my mind the Menzies Bay property was crucial to our business.

AN UNEXPECTED CURVE BALL

Shortly after launching the *Marine Link #II* we had a nasty encounter with the PST (Provincial Sales Tax) auditor. During the construction of the *ML#II,* Jenkins Marine had omitted charging us the PST. Jenkins had been audited and the auditor simply followed the "blood trail" to MLT. As my business acumen was not sufficiently honed at that point, this caught us completely unawares. The result was a $50,000 bill for taxes not paid, penalties and accrued interest. It was a case of interpretation between Jenkins and the provincial sales tax auditors, which led me to spend more "good money chasing the bad" when we decided to appeal the case.

I was referred to a PST specialist over in Vancouver who proved to be rather unscrupulous. At my first appointment I was greeted by him asking me, "How's business?" This was code for the real intent, "Can you pay my bill?" I am sure he looked at Marine Link Transportation and myself as country bumpkins. During our first meeting in his office he took great pains to assure me that there were three or four viable avenues of appeal concerning our PST circumstances. Four or five months of interaction provided absolutely no result and I am sure that no effort was expended other than to make out our sizeable bill, followed shortly thereafter by another bill, which I refused to pay. Suffice it to say my ability to write a letter extracted us from this situation. I ended up with a bad taste in my mouth which persists to this day. Our bank account remained intact but we were still stuck with the PST bill. Ten years later the same PST auditor phoned me and said, "It's time to do it again"—meaning another audit. All they realized this time around was $250, hardly worth the auditor's time.

JOHN JENKINS, AN EXTRAORDINARY SHIPBUILDER

In the 1980s and 1990s if you were looking around Victoria for a boat builder or repairer, particularly if your boat was of wood construction, chances were that you would end up at Jenkins Marine. Eventually you would find the "landlocked" yard at the end of Erskine Lane.[1] Driving into that yard you would wonder if it was the right place because it certainly didn't look like a shipyard. Yet, Jenkins Marine is the sole remaining shipyard of any size outside of Victoria Shipyard in Esquimalt and Point Hope Shipyard in Victoria's Inner Harbour. It is unique in that it has never gone through reorganization, creditor protection or receivership. In short, John Jenkins is a survivor and for good reason—he is an outstanding problem solver, a trained shipwright and an extremely practical thinker, all of which prompts me to say that if I ever "crash and burn" in the boat business, or anything marine for that matter, I want John at my side.

John has a long association with Marine Link beginning with trucking the *Togian* from Ootsa Lake to Victoria. *(see p.13)* Jenkins Marine was awarded the contract to build the *Marine Link #II* in 1988. Two years later, John flew with me to Fort McMurray to inspect the *Aurora Explorer* which at the time was in the dryland storage of its owner, A-Frame Contracting. *(see p.66)* Jenkins Marine undertook the three-dimensional reconstruction of the *Aurora Explorer* through the winter of 1998–99 and has since done extensive modifications on both *Marine Link #II* and the *Aurora Explorer* for their new owners.

A shipyard is the last place on earth where a small boat or ship owner wants to be if the intent is to maintain a budget and get value for money. *(see "The Shipyard Walk," p.113)* However, I learned early in the game that if John Jenkins looked at the naval architect's drawings and said, "It won't work," one best pay attention because chances are high that indeed it won't work, but John will devise some new design that will. Unfortunately there are fewer and fewer craftsmen like John Jenkins in today's world.

1. In 2014 the Jenkins yard moved to the former site of Sooke Marine Industries (Maywell Wickham) on Kaltasin Road in Sooke, BC.

Al and Tim on the bow ramp of *ML#II.* No "suits" here. These guys actually get their hands dirty!

Tim *(l)* and Al with Dick Meadows, Al's father, in the MLT freight yard.

Chapter 6

A STORY WORTH TELLING

A brand new *ML#II* in Caviar Cove, Drury Inlet, unloading a gravel truck. This is a perfect example of a ro-ro (roll-on/roll-off) operation.

The year was 1989 and we were still at Tyee Spit. *ML#I* and *ML#II* were fully engaged with supply and service to silviculture and logging camps as well as transporting fish food for the fish farms. We also continued with many other regular freight accounts. With the *ML#II* now part of the fleet, Tim and I needed to hire additional skippers. The first skipper hired was Greg Janes, followed by Philippe Menetrier, both excellent employees. Greg retired in 2003 and Philippe has been with MLT for over twenty-five years.

As the Sunshine Coast area was being abandoned, new fish farm sites were opened, particularly to the north of Campbell River. The major fish food manufacturers were now consolidated on the lower mainland. One was Ewos, a Swedish-controlled company located in Surrey in the Fraser Valley, and the other was Moore-Clark, who had a plant located on the north arm of the Fraser River in South Vancouver. Moore Clark was a subsidiary of Nutreco, a world-wide producer of animal feeds and an offshoot of oil giant British Petroleum. There was also Whitecrest Mills located in the industrial park north of Campbell River, which soon went out of business. Today, all of this is consolidated into one large entity known as Marine Harvest Canada and almost all fish food volumes are handled by bulk barges towed from Vancouver.

New freight opportunities came our way in 1990–91. One of these was delivery of bulk propane to fishing lodges, logging camps and coastal communities, marketed under Premier Propane, which is now part of Superior Propane. Additionally, our business included delivering explosives for Conex Explosives, later known as Orica, previously part of the CIL group (Canadian Industries Limited). Eventually the propane business proved unprofitable due to the constant high cost of training crews and maintenance of equipment.

HIRING EX-FISHERMEN

Throughout the hiring process at Marine Link, Tim and I agreed that the best source of new employees was former commercial salmon trollers or individuals who were previously self-employed. Intuitively, we both knew they had the skill set necessary to solve operational problems, they were resilient and they were able to adapt to changing circumstances. Invariably, they had the gift of the gab and the lore of the coast. While employing upwards of thirty-five employees at the peak of our business in 1999, half of our employee complement had a background in the fishing industry.

Alvin Tye is the forklift driver central to the following testimonial which was written by Vic Sosnowsky. Alvin is a superb problem solver.

Here is an example of a problem solver and a customer's testimonial that bears out the quality of employee that Marine Link was able to attract. The testimonial comes from Vic Sosnowsky, a Vancouver-area building contractor. MLT first got to know him in 1992. When I recently told Vic I was in the process of writing this book, he was delighted and remarked, "That story has to be told." He went on to ask if he could contribute to the book by sharing his own family's experience with the *Aurora Explorer*. On the following pages is Vic's remembrance of a delivery in 1998.

A CUSTOMER'S TESTIMONIAL

It was with great anticipation and excitement that Cathy, Woldy and I stood on the beach of our first wilderness property at Hemming Bay, East Thurlow Island, awaiting the arrival of Marine Link's first delivery. It was mid-July 1998. Rounding Brougham Point, still a mere speck on the horizon was the Aurora Explorer. *We could hear the steady high pitched drone of her twin diesels. Woldy and I along with several helpers and friends of Alex's, had spent the last four days in Marine Link's staging yard organizing and packaging the contents of a 60-foot semi-trailer, a flatdeck truck and a large single-axle moving van into 33 totes (4'x4' to 4'x 8' shipping containers, built on site). The shipment consisted of years of saved materials recycled from my building jobs, doors, windows, memorabilia, building materials and hardware from our father's estate, bricks, cement and mortar for a four-flue chimney, lifts of plywood and new lumber, plus a prefab, 1,800 square foot building in packable sections. While we were putting all this together, Guy, the yard manager came by and asked, "What are you guys building up there, a commune?" This was the culmination of twenty years of dreaming, discussions and planning for our joint family retreat. As the* Aurora *neared the beach, we could hear the chatter of the bridge deck radio and the mate on the bow gave instructions to the skipper as they made a safe landing. "Is this Hemming Bay?" the mate joked. "We've got a couple of things to drop off." The ramp came down, ship's crew fired up forklifts and cranes, orders were yelled above the noise of machinery. The invasion had begun. It felt like D-day at Omaha Beach.*

Down came a monster 4-wheel drive articulated forklift with the first load. Alvin, the driver, yelled over the noise of the engine, "Where d'ya wan'er?" The machine lurched and with wheels spinning as it climbed up the uneven beach and lowered its load exactly where directed. The first half-dozen loads went like clockwork. "This is gonna be a piece of cake," I thought. Then a half hour into the operation, on its way back for another load, the forklift suddenly stopped to everyone's surprise. Alvin, the driver, tried several times to restart the machine, but to no avail. "Well, isn't that a nice howdy-do, I guess we'll have to change the fuel filter. No problem. We always keep a spare taped to the steering column under the dash," Upon inspection, he came back scratching his head. "Well, I'll be . . .," was his remark. The last guy who changed the filter didn't replace it. I'll check the log book when we get back and have a word with whoever that was, but right now we have to improvise." This was a serious show stopper situation. "Do you have a five-gallon bucket, a piece of half-inch hose and a hose clamp? We're gonna set up a direct syphon and bypass the filter." Bucket and hose clamp were supplied. "Next," he says, "we'll have to secure the bucket to the cab roof." Bungies and rope were fetched. Next, he removed the filter mounted on the engine, placed one end of the hose into the bucket on the cab roof securing it with some tape so it wouldn't fall out once the siphon was set up. Then putting the other hose end into his mouth, he began to suck out a mouthful of diesel fuel. The hose end was pinched and then clamped directly to the fuel pump. Now all was ready for priming. In order to do this each one of the four injectors had to be taken off individually, hand pumped via the hand primer pump till fuel squirted out and quickly screwed back in so as not to get any air in the system, Diesel was squirting and dripping everywhere. This entire operation took approximately 30 minutes. Alvin methodically went about the entire procedure without any muttering or signs of frustration. He remained amazingly calm, cool as a cucumber and not a foul word left his mouth.

Climbing back into the cab, he said, "She should go now." He hit the start button and the diesel sprung to life. Thumbs up and we were back in business.

Once the machine was running again, the off-loading continued with amazing speed. When it became too dark to see, lights came on and lift after lift was brought up and placed on the building site. The machine did stop several times due to the siphon being broken and air getting into the line. Each time the priming procedure had to be repeated in sequence and its entirety. Alvin did this time and again without complaint, even though he ended up soaked from head to toe from the fuel sloshing around on top of the cab. The delivery complete and all the delivery equipment back on board, the Aurora *hoisted her ramp and backed away from the beach. Woldy, Cathy and I yelled our gratitude and goodbyes, all amazed at what had just transpired, in spite of a setback that could have kaiboshed the whole operation. Those guys were AWESOME! Our hats off to them, especially Alvin.*

Cheers
Vic (Vic Sosnowsky)

AN INCIDENT WITH MARINE LINK #II

In 1991 the *Marine Link #II* was involved in a severe incident but it served to confirm that the vessel was very well built. The boat had been loaded with eighty tons of bagged and palletized fish food, bound for a fish farm in Okisollo Channel. The trip was considered a "milk run" in sheltered waters, with an anticipated time frame of about ten hours there and back to our base. On this day, the early spring weather was particularly bad, with driving rain in a stiff southeast wind, all of which made for greatly reduced visibility particularly as most of the trip and delivery at the farm would take place during the night. The master, Greg Janes, was a very experienced and competent boat handler. The western entrance to Okisollo Channel is narrow and confined but easily navigated at night with the aid of radar.

Using the radar, Greg had turned the *ML#II* into the channel while the visibility ahead was almost zero in the rain and darkness. Suddenly, without any warning, the fully loaded boat travelling at seven knots ran into a rock bluff. The impact was so severe that mate Tom Brugiom, lying in his bunk at the time, was hurled forward cracking his head on the wall. All the galley cupboards flew open hurling their contents onto the galley floor in a huge mess of broken glass. The pallets of fish food collapsed into a heap on the cargo deck. After a thorough inspection of the hull and compartments for flooding, Greg was able to bring the damaged boat back to base.

The boat had survived the accident but had sustained a huge dent in the hull just below the hinge of the bow ramp. This dent measured 7' across by 4' vertically with the hull plate pushed in to a depth of 8". The collision void was a scene of mangled steel, but miraculously there was no breach of the hull and no one was seriously hurt.

Further investigation found that the radar set being used had gone into "lock-up." This is a situation when the image on the display does not update the position of the boat relative to other targets, in this case the near shoreline. Shortly after, Transport Canada issued a safety notice to shipping warning vessel operators of this defect. Larger ships typically run two radars at the same time, in part to detect when this dangerous situation occurs.

Few vessels would have survived this accident intact as the *ML#II* had. When the boat was built, John Jenkins had added additional bracing and stiffening in the collision void, as he was not happy with the naval architect drawings. This additional strength probably saved the *ML#II* from much more serious damage. Our estimated cost to repair the boat was $80,000 with a $10,000 deductible on our insurance policy and who knows how much time out of service if taken to a shipyard.

Art Peltonen, one of MLT's senior maintenance staff, seen here taking a break while one of MLT's vessels was in dry dock.

MLT had a history of doing most of its repairs and vessel improvements with "in-house" staff or contractors, as we did in this case. We often used tidal grids in Alert Bay, Campbell River and Fanny Bay, usually working at night in the winter low tides. We did repairs with our own maintenance staff, probably saving hundreds of thousands of dollars over the years by not having to go to a shipyard.

Sometimes this was unavoidable, but if we could avoid it we did. The *ML#II* was dewatered on the tidal grid at Fanny Bay just a few kilometres south of Courtenay

Gary Irwin currently lives in Black Creek on Vancouver Island, where he creates superb metal sculptures. We first met Gary as part of the Jenkins Marine crew building the *ML#II*. *(Jo Irwin photo)*

and the repair to the bow was undertaken during the low-water intervals. MLT called upon the expertise of Gary Irwin to head-man the repair. Like John Jenkins, Gary is one of a kind and the best steel fitter that we have ever worked with. Lying on his back in a hollow dug out beneath the boat, Gary cut away the damaged hull plating and, over a period of about seven days, fitted and welded new steel.

It is this type of excellent tradesman which MLT was consistently able to tap into and which significantly contributed to our success.[1]

In 1997 the *ML#II* was sold to Stolt Sea Farms, now part of Marine Harvest Canada. The name changed to *Atlantic Harvester,* with First Nations personnel from Alert Bay as crew. Unfortunately, *Atlantic Harvester* sank in Discovery Passage just west of Campbell River on the evening of October 18, 2014, with the tragic loss of two of her crew members.

GUY ADAMS JOINS MARINE LINK TRANSPORTATION

When I served on the board of directors of the Pacific Trollers Association I got to know Guy Adams who was on the board with me. I recognized in Guy a sharp mind and the ability to juggle multiple pieces of information and tasks at one time. I made him an offer to become a full-time MLT employee, which he accepted. He sold his troller, *BC Tuna,* and has been with us ever since.

When Philippe Menetrier or Greg Janes were unavailable, Guy skippered the *ML#II*. Later, Guy came ashore permanently as our freight dispatcher.

Guy Adams, dispatcher for Marine Link at our office on Tyee Spit. (circa 1995)

Marine Link #II stuck in ice at Mereworth Sound, part of the Seymour Inlet system. Philippe Menetrier is holding a piece of ice 6" thick. (1993) *(Mike Pinch collection)*

Skipper Greg Janes *(l)* and mate Philippe Menetrier at the end of the line. The ice is thick enough to hold their weight. *(Mike Pinch collection)*

1. *(opposite page)* The reader may wonder why we simply did not initiate an insurance claim to cover the repair cost of the *ML#II.* To do so meant that the vessel would have had to go to a shipyard, where the repair costs and lost time would have been significantly greater. As well, MLT would have had to pay the deductible on the policy in any event and would lose its claim-free status, resulting in higher premium costs in the future. Our outlook was that insurance policies were in place and should be reserved for the "big hits" such as a total loss of a vessel.

Marine Link #II loading a large cargo of construction material.

Our new office on Tyee Spit when we started our passenger business. This building served in part as our passenger reception lounge. (circa 1990)

Chapter 7

THE PURCHASING AND COMMISSIONING OF THE AURORA EXPLORER

In the foreground, *Aurora Explorer* in Discovery Passage with a large cruise ship behind. Bigger is not necessarily better. Our goal in purchasing the *Aurora Explorer* was to offer an alternative experience—an adventure cruise well off the beaten track where a large cruise ship will never go.

A CRITICAL OBSERVATION

While operating the *ML#I* and *ML#II* for freight, Tim and I often invited interested friends along for a trip or two. On one trip on the *ML#I,* I invited good friend John Hurley. I anticipated the trip as a one- or two-day run but once we were underway the phone kept ringing and the work kept coming and the trip became seven or eight days. John still reminds me of this although he enjoyed it thoroughly, as did other friends who came along. I began to realize that this was a real adventure for our invited guests even though at times it was bad weather and hard work.

Historically, carrying passengers on the coast by ship was strictly for transportation, in order to supply and connect the outport communities that dotted the coastal waters of BC. This was during the era of the CPR

Princess ships (1900–1955) and the Union Steamship Company ships (1889–1958). As well, Northland Navigation (1944–1976) had a regular freight supply service from its Vancouver base up the coast as far as Prince Rupert. A limited number of passengers could purchase staterooms on the Northland run, but it was essentially a freight and supply voyage, not an adventure cruise.

Always on the lookout for new revenue streams, I recognized that freight and passengers could be married in a landing craft-type vessel. Such a ship would have the ro-ro capacity and a cargo-deck area and superstructure necessary for both purposes.

CONFUSION ABOUNDS OVER PASSENGER-CARRYING VESSELS

There was an essential complication here that one could not lose sight of—we were contemplating berthed passengers (stay over night on the vessel) as compared to day-trip passengers who do not remain on the vessel overnight. Charter vessels are under yet a different regulatory regime. Typically, a charter involves a single customer who is hiring the boat, although it may be multi-days in duration and with berthed clientele. The International Maritime Organization (IMO), to which Canada is signatory, does not consider a charter to be a passenger-carrying situation. So long as the *Aurora Explorer* carries no more than twelve passengers, she is technically not considered a passenger-carrying vessel. In spite of this confusion, she must still comply with all the regulatory requirements of a passenger ship.

In 1990, I set about looking for a suitable vessel knowing there probably would be few worthwhile prospects. However, luck was on our side and I discovered that a Vancouver boat brokerage was listing a potentially suitable landing craft vessel in northern Alberta. It was named the *Aurora Explorer*[1] and had been put up for sale by its owner, Andy Frame of A-Frame Contracting in Fort McMurray.

I again engaged John Jenkins and we flew to Fort McMurray. We went to the A-Frame Contracting yard[2] to survey the *Aurora Explorer* in dryland storage where she had been for about three years. Andy had previously used her on the Clearwater and Athabasca Rivers to move all types of freight, including full-sized houses that he had bought surplus from Radium City when the uranium mine shut down. Andy was a very imposing individual whose skill and energy were evident in the many business ventures he had undertaken on the waterways of northern Alberta and the Northwest Territories.

When John and I surveyed the *Aurora* we found that she was not in the best condition;

1. The *Aurora Explorer* and her sister ship *Aurora Surveyor* were prefabricated in sections in Edmonton, Alberta. These sections were then trucked to Hay River in the Northwest Territories for assembly. The builder of the *Aurora* was Kapps Trucking of Hay River and it was Kapps who put the *Aurora* to work in the Mackenzie River delta and later sold it to Andy Frame. The *Aurora* was about twenty years old when Marine Link Transportation purchased her.
2. In 1990 the A-Frame Contracting yard was not in downtown Fort McMurray but it was close, as was the muddy Athabasca River. In 2011 when Holly and I went to visit our daughter who was working and going to school in Fort McMurray, all traces of the A-Frame yard had disappeared and that address was a Canadian Tire store.

the scantlings were on the light side and much of the apparatus and gear, including the engines, were obsolete. Nevertheless, there were some essential elements: she had a landing craft/barge-type hull which we could easily modify and enough superstructure space to fit improved passenger staterooms. The staterooms and galley had provided sufficient accommodation for her original operations (conducting seismic surveys in the Mackenzie River delta), but the stall-type washrooms and metal bunks needed to go.

In the "big picture" the *Aurora Explorer* had the basic parameters we knew were essential to convert the vessel into roll-on/roll-off freight as well as carriage of berthed passengers. Fundamentally, what the *Aurora Explorer* represented was an existing hull, which had previously been surveyed and certified by Transport Canada Ship Safety. I knew this was immeasurably valuable in that the vessel was already in the system and we were not faced with having to import a hull. That allowed for upgrading and modification within boundaries that were affordable and which could be staged over time. To build the same vessel from the keel up, brand new, would probably have cost four times as much, which was beyond our financial capability. There was considerable "intrinsic value" in the hull not obviously apparent to the casual observer.

Tim and I and John Jenkins weighed the merits and demerits of our purchasing the *Aurora Explorer.* We decided to go for it and shortly after arrived at a purchase/sale agreement with Andy Frame. One of the key provisions required delivery of the vessel intact to Campbell River. This proved to be an arduous undertaking that very nearly came to a disaster at Point Barrow, Alaska.

A STEP BACK IN TIME 1967

I digress now to early July in 1967 when, as a nineteen year old, I departed Victoria on the CSS *Richardson* as a deckhand; our destination was Tuktoyaktuk in Canada's western Arctic. The *Richardson* was being transferred there for hydrographic survey work, just ahead of what was to become the big oil and gas exploration push in the western Arctic by a multitude of companies, one of which was Dome Petroleum.

The journey was uneventful until we arrived at Dutch Harbour in the Aleutian Islands, a former US military installation in WWII. This abandoned base was gigantic and went on as far as the eye could see. We departed Dutch Harbour in flat calm weather on our way to cross the Bering Sea. Our captain, Tom McCulloch of Victoria, was clearly worried that the favourable sea conditions would not last. The *Richardson* was a small vessel, just 66' in length, with a crew of seven (captain, mate, engineer, cook, bo'sun and two deckhands).

By the time we reached the Pribilof Islands we were in a raging seventy-knot storm. We were fortunate in having the rough sea on our stern and twenty-four hours later we arrived at Port Clarence, Alaska, just south of the Bering Strait. Here we took on fuel which had been cached on shore by our support ship, the Canadian Coast Guard icebreaker *Camsell,* which was three days ahead of us.

Passing through the Bering Strait into the Chukchi Sea, the *Richardson* set course for Point Barrow which was some two days away. Captain McCulloch was fully expecting to encounter ice conditions, but we hoped that it would not be solid ice and would allow us to work our way through by following open-water leads in the ice. About halfway to Point Barrow the first ice floes began to appear and conditions became progressively worse as we observed less and less open water. Our progress was slowed and eventually we ran out of leads to follow. Conditions deteriorated quickly, with a stiff onshore wind that was ominous. We hoped that the ice pack would break up, but instead it began to form pressure ridges where large floes were pancaked on top of one another as the onshore wind brought more floes down on us.

Our situation was becoming grave as the *Richardson* was completely immobilized and even though the boat had an ice-strengthened hull we were worried it would be crushed altogether. McCulloch had just advised the *Camsell*[3] by radio that we may be in need of assistance when suddenly the *Richardson* was lifted clear out of the water and put on her side at a 35° list to starboard. McCulloch broadcast a mayday call, the first of his long career at sea. The *Camsell* responded to the mayday and indicated they were coming to our assistance from the east —but they were at least three days away.

The USCG icebreaker *Northwind*[4] also responded to the mayday and was coming to our assistance from the west where she had been patrolling near the Russian shore. Thus began three days of sleeping on deck (in twenty-four-hour daylight), eating sandwiches and hoping that the boat would not capsize. I recall that from time to time a DC-3 aircraft would come out and circle us just to confirm that we were still there. By the fourth day the *Northwind* and the *Camsell* were both within sight, but they were making minimal progress through the pressure ice. On day four the *Camsell*'s helicopter, a Bell two-seater, landed beside the *Richardson* bringing the *Camsell*'s captain to consult with Captain McCulloch.

Eventually the *Northwind* got to us first, passing slowly by, relieving the pressure of the ice on the *Richardson.* Her crew lined the guard rails, cheering that they had won the race over the *Camsell.* The *Richardson* was towed out of the ice by the *Camsell* and sustained much additional damage due to chunks of ice from the propeller wash of the *Camsell* striking our hull.

Eventually we gained open water where the *Richardson'*s damaged propeller was changed, allowing us to continue under our own power. We made for Tuktoyaktuk where the US Navy had a floating dry dock on loan to Canada. We remained there for the next three weeks for repairs. In the dry dock the *Richardson* was dwarfed by the size of the dock. Once repaired, we spent the remainder of August and September on hydrographic survey in the Beaufort Sea. The ship was then winterized and moored in the harbour to overwinter in the ice. The crew flew home to Victoria. It had been quite an adventure for a nineteen-year-old.[5]

The *Richardson* is stuck hard in the ice at Point Barrow, listing 20° to starboard.

The *Richardson* is temporarily on an even keel, but mostly lifted out of the water.

The USCG icebreaker *Northwind* is breaking heavy pressure ice, about 1 km (.6 mi) away from the *Richardson.*

The *Northwind* is close in to the *Richardson* with most of its crew lining the decks cheering that they got there first.

(opposite page)
3. The *Camsell* was a medium-sized buoy tender of about 2,000 tons, fitted with an icebreaker bow. She had a crew of fifty-seven and was based in Victoria, BC.
4. The *Northwind* was a "Wind" class icebreaker of about 4,000 tons, one of three such ships in the US Coast Guard at the time. She had a crew of 219 and was based in Seattle, WA.
5. In 1968 I returned for a second summer as a deckhand on the *Richardson*, this time flying both ways. Once the ice went out of the harbour at Tuktoyaktuk the *Richardson* spent July through September conducting hydrographic survey in the Beaufort Sea.

Northwind passing the *Richardson*. Note the helicopter hangar and funnel. At the base of the funnel is a landing craft on davits, similar to the *Togian* we purchased at Ootsa Lake in 1978. *(see p.12–13)*

Al Meadows standing on the bow of the *Richardson* while in dry dock at Tuktoyaktuk.

THE EPIC VOYAGE OF THE AURORA EXPLORER 1990

The epic voyage of the *Aurora Explorer* from Fort McMurray, Alberta, to Campbell River, BC, in the summer of 1990 would warrant a book in its own right. The journey began in May at the A-Frame Contracting yard on the Clearwater River. Once the ice broke up in the river, the *Aurora Explorer* was launched. She proceeded downstream on the Athabasca River, then across Lake Athabasca and entered the Slave River. At Fort Smith, midway down the Slave River, a 24 km (14 mi) stretch of rapids required portaging the boat over land and around the rapids. Brute force was needed, given the bulk and weight of the ship.

We had intended to send a purchaser's representative on the delivery trip, but at the last moment we decided against it. As a result, we did not have someone on board to document and photograph this gigantic feat. We can surmise that the vessel was pulled sideways out of the river over logs that were placed forming a skidway up onto the adjacent road. Then log skids were aligned fore and aft under the hull and a D-8 bulldozer pulled the assembly down the gravel road with another bulldozer working ahead to trim the road up as necessary. This was done over the 24 km distance and once below the rapids the *Aurora* was launched back into the river, again sliding down skid logs that had been placed for the purpose. The entire portage probably took five to six days. The voyage continued and, as the reader will see from the fold-out map at the back of the book, it was a long, long way down the Slave and Mackenzie Rivers. Once at the delta of the Mackenzie and upon entering the Beaufort Sea, the *Aurora* detoured to Tuktoyaktuk for fuel and reprovisioning.

Setting out again, the vessel transited the Beaufort Sea onto the Alaskan north slope where everything leads to Point Barrow. This prominent point of land is the "pinch" location where all navigation either succeeds or fails, depending on ice and wind conditions. If you can't round Point Barrow you are stuck, and stuck good. If the prevailing wind is onshore the ice blocks navigation, whereas if the wind is offshore open "leads" in the ice allow vessels to carry on.

It was déjà vu! I remembered my trip on the *Richardson* some thirty years before. The memory was replayed, in reverse, with the *Aurora Explorer* barely rounding Point Barrow on her way to BC.

The remainder of the delivery trip was uneventful and after a more than ninety-day journey the *Aurora* arrived in Campbell River. At that point we completed the purchase with Andy Frame and took ownership of the boat. *(see fold-out map)*

Had the *Aurora* not made it around Point Barrow the story of MLT would have been very different.

Two views of the *Aurora Explorer.* The top photograph shows her in dryland storage in the A-Frame yard at Fort McMurray in 1990; the lower photo shows her, post-reconstruction, underway in Bute Inlet in 1999. The "sow's ear" had been turned into a "silk purse."

THE BEGINNING OF OUR PASSENGER TRADE

With the purchase of the *Aurora Explorer* in 1990 we were eager to get it into condition to begin our passenger business. Having a significant in-house maintenance and repair capacity, we set about immediately refitting our new acquisition.

Men like Bruce Stockand and John Jenkins, who had served their apprenticeship in boat building, represent a quality of skill that is difficult to find today. These were master shipwrights and craftsmen who could repair anything and build anything. Bruce was the *Aurora Explorer*'s first engineer and head-manned most of the upgrading work, together with Tim. The *Aurora* was completely rewired by Victoria Marine Electric; also installed was an automatic sprinkler system throughout the boat. Facilities were upgraded in the staterooms and the stall toilets gave way to modern washroom and shower facilities.

This refitting[6] took place between 1990 and 1992. During this time the *Aurora* was employed in transporting freight but was laid up for interior improvements during the winter months. All of this was under the watchful eye of Transport Canada Ship Safety and included upgrading of the lifeboat/life-raft capacity, the automatic fire-suppression system in the engine room, new watertight bulkheads in the interior of the ship and hard-wired smoke and flooding alarms, complete with a warning panel on the bridge. In addition, the certification of the *Aurora* crew was enhanced through further training in marine emergency, such as life-boat/life-raft and firefighting procedures.

In the summer of 1992, we began a pilot program of carrying passengers on board the *Aurora*. Passenger capacity was eight in four double-occupancy staterooms.

As work progressed on the *Aurora Explorer*[7] we began to consider how we might market our new adventure cruise. We considered different venues, including travel industry trade shows. Bruce made up a display assembly which I packed off to a number of travel shows, often with Holly or good friend Vern Logan as helpers and, on occasion, my dad. We participated in shows in Toronto, Calgary, Seattle and Vancouver where we enjoyed significant interest from the fifty-five-plus age group. Retired seniors were definitely our market demographic and I would not hand out a brochure to anyone who did not have grey hair.

I had developed the slogan "Explore the Working Coast" which keyed well on our clientele. Above all else I targeted travel writers, which paid off in an extraordinary amount of media exposure throughout North America and Europe. Major stories about the *Aurora Explorer* appeared in the pages of the *Los Angeles Times, Times of London, The Chicago Tribune, Beautiful*

6. The *Aurora Explorer* had a Sperry Rand gyro compass for navigation as the standard magnetic compass is unreliable in northern latitudes. This sizeable instrument was surplus to our needs and MLT donated it to Camosun College Interurban Campus in Victoria to assist teaching in the marine training program there.

7. Many people wonder why a ship operating out of Campbell River, BC, has Edmonton as port of registry on its stern. The *Aurora Explorer* is registered in Edmonton, Alberta, because it was fabricated there. Edmonton is the registry serving vessels operating in the NWT and the Western Arctic.

BC Magazine as well as the front page of *The Vancouver Sun,* to name a few.

We were surprised and elated in 1996 when representatives of BC's Knowledge Network contacted us about producing a five-minute vignette on the *Aurora Explorer* for *BC Moments*. This particular episode was the most popular *BC Moments* ever produced. It was unprecedented when, in 2002, the Network proposed creating a sequel—which became the eight-minute *BC Moments* entitled "Aurora's Working Coast."

At the time, marketing was a totally new business action for me and I often called on the experience of people in the tourism industry. I remember the advice, renewed on an annual basis by good friend Harvey Lee. At the time, Harvey was the owner of the Vancouver franchise for Gray Line Tours. He was instrumental in refining the experience on the *Aurora* and for years kept telling me, "You're too cheap. Your price isn't high enough." Tim, Guy and myself had no idea what the value of the experience was because to us it was just more water and trees. I learned quickly.

The *Aurora Explorer* is now owned by our former MLT partner Guy Adams, and is as popular as ever, typically sold out well in advance of the upcoming season. The name "Aurora Explorer" is unique and has its own cachet.

The Marine Link fleet: *Aurora Explorer* in the foreground, *ML#II* and *ML#I*. (circa 1992)

Chapter 8

MANAGING GROWTH

Our business was growing and Tim and I recognized that there was an opportunity to expand our sphere of operation into the central coast region, particularly Rivers Inlet. In the summer months the Rivers Inlet, Hakai Pass and Namu area was the location of a dozen seasonal fishing lodges. There was also significant logging activity in Moses Inlet, Kilbella Bay and around Doc Creek in the Burke Channel area, and on up to Bella Coola. With the *Aurora Explorer* and *ML#II* having only limited capacity, we went looking for an additional landing craft platform that could make longer runs with a greater freight capacity.

THE WORKHORSE OF THE FLEET: mv A.G. FORD
(formerly, Richmond Carrier)

We had long admired a competitor, Bob Behan, who had built and operated the landing craft mv *Richmond Carrier*. In 1992 we approached Behan and were successful in purchasing the vessel. This particular landing craft was built largely to satisfy a contract with Boom Chain Transportation Ltd. (BCT) situated on the north arm of the Fraser River directly underneath the Knight Street Bridge. Boom Chain was an interesting outfit, essentially a co-operative of the major logging companies (MacMillan Bloedel, Weldwood Canada, Crown Zellerbach, Western Forest Products and others). Its purpose was to act as a central inventory of boom gear consisting of boom chain, swifter wires and bundling wires, which make up a boom of logs. This boom gear was collected after disassembly from the boom of logs at the mill. At BCT the cables and chains were inspected, repaired and then redistributed upcoast to the logging operations of the co-op members. The *Richmond Carrier* was the link between BCT and these logging operations. *(see p.76)* In addition, the BCT yard served as a depot for general freight sourced from Vancouver for transport to upcoast locations.

Jim Buttar, manager of BCT, came knocking on our door in Campbell River and we negotiated an arrangement to carry on as the marine distributor of BCT's materials. This was a profitable arrangement for MLT as the ship would typically load 250 tons of boom gear every two weeks.

The *Richmond Carrier* won additional market share for MLT and was the means to grow our operational territory significantly. With this new addition to the fleet, I felt it was necessary for our management to have the

BOOM GEAR DESCRIBED

(by Syd Heal)

"Boom Gear" is the common term used to describe all the chain and cables used to assemble and hold together a boom of logs in preparation and during the time a tug tows the boom to a mill. Such a tow will likely include an intermediate stop in storage grounds until final delivery at the mill site where the boom will be broken up and logs prepared for milling into lumber. Towing of log flat booms can be a risky business if the weather, particularly wind velocity, wave height and ocean currents have to be contended with. As a consequence, the boom has to be strong enough to withstand these forces.

There are two common types of booms. The first is the traditional flat boom that was used in the nineteenth century, where floating logs were coralled loosely into squared sections formed by swifter logs at the sides and crossbeams or spreaders positioned to enable each square or section to retain its shape and structural strength. These specially manufactured short lengths of heavy chain, fitted at both ends with a special joining device, are used to tie the swifter logs together, end to end, and it is these chains and their devices that are the main concern in this description.

The other type of boom, a development of the late twentieth century, is known as a bundle boom, which is literally many bundles of logs that are parcelled together on shore at the log booming ground operated by the logging company. The bundling machine is big enough to hold a full load from a logging truck while they are strapped together with heavy-duty galvanized wire of predetermined length and then skidded sideways straight into the water. Here they are pushed into a pocket or corral similar to that used when assembling flat booms.

Probably about seven-eighths of the bundle boom is under water, whereas a flat boom, a single layer of logs floating on the surface, draws very little water. With so many of the logs beneath the surface, bundle booms require a far greater draft and a more powerful tug to tow them, but probably contain ten to twenty times more logs than that of the flat boom for the same surface area. Flat boom towing is hardly known today and, with the changing technology involved, Boom Chain Transportation eventually went out of business. Boom chains and swifter wires typically provided 8–12 cycles of reuse before being scrapped, whereas bundling wire is used only once before being recycled via the scrapyard.

A Marine Link forklift carrying a lift of boom chains.

The Boom Chain Transportation yard on Mitchell Island is full of various piles of boom gear. The concrete pillars shown here are supports for the Knight Street bridge in Vancouver.

appropriate certification. I took a two-year hiatus as general manager of operations for MLT and returned to school at Camosun College in Victoria and Pacific Marine Training Institute in Vancouver, which is now part of BCIT. With my commercial fishing and *Richardson* time I had the requisite sea time to qualify to take the watchkeeping mate's certificate. After that certification, I continued and graduated in 1994 with my master's command endorsement ticket to captain a vessel of 500 tons or less.

This "ticketing" formally secured the legal requirements and training specified by Transport Canada to operate MLT's vessels. Tim then embarked on a session at school as well and secured his watchkeeping mate's ticket. During this time we hired Ford Cannon as our general manager for the business.

Al Meadows is presented with a new ship's clock by his aunt, Lin Ford, at the renaming of the *Richmond Carrier* as the *A.G. Ford.*

In 1997 I renamed the *Richmond Carrier* to honour my uncle, Commander Alan Geoffrey Ford (a career naval officer), who had passed away suddenly in 1992. The vessel was named mv *A.G. Ford* in a formal christening including a naval padre and all the requisite ceremony. It included breaking a bottle of champagne over the new name painted on the bow and my aunt, Lin Ford, presented the ship with a new clock.

The *A.G. Ford* operated for many years as the workhorse of MLT, ably skippered by Greg Janes or Philippe Menetrier. Greg retired in 2003 and Philippe continues as one of the senior skippers of the *Aurora Explorer.* We sold the *A.G. Ford* in 2005 as we downsized our business plan and reoriented to tug and barge operations.

Landing craft are regulated as crewed ships, so the *A.G. Ford* carried a five-man crew, whereas a tug and barge usually can be operated with a crew of three or fewer. A barge can carry 50 percent more cargo than the corresponding landing craft. The economics of the two clearly showed that the cost of operation and maintenance of landing craft compared poorly to the corresponding tug and barge operation. We later purchased the barge *Coastal Roamer* as our new business plan emerged.

The *A.G. Ford* continues operating in Nootka Sound for Nootka Sound Services based out of Gold River.

Richmond Carrier, before being renamed *A.G. Ford,* off-loading at a logging camp in Rivers Inlet. In taking this photo I had to skirt around the landing into adjoining bush and found myself walking through a Chinese cemetery. Obviously this was the site of a former cannery, which employed many Chinese, dating back to the early part of the twentieth century.

(above) Bob Olsen at the helm of the *A.G. Ford.*

(left) Mate Mike Pratt operating the hydraulic controls of the main crane on board the *A.G. Ford.*

VERTICAL MOBILE UNITS

In 1992 we were granted certification from Transport Canada to carry passengers ("vertical mobile units") and in June of that year the *Aurora Explorer* embarked her first passengers. The passenger complement was eight in four bunkbed-style staterooms. In that first year of operation we carried passengers for twelve trips during the season spanning July and August. The passenger side of the business is conducted under the name "Marine Link Tours."

Our first cook was Wendy Deluca who had a real passion for cooking. Wendy was many things besides a creative cook, as she undertook the tasks of provisioning, staffing and administration of passenger services. Around the same time we hired Donna Sawatsky as the alternate trip cook. She retired in 2012 after twenty years with MLT.

Wendy Deluca. (circa 2000)

Donna Sawatsky *(r)*, cook, with Gena Sandberg, steward. (circa 2002)

A MAJOR INCIDENT WITH THE AURORA EXPLORER

In 1996 the *Aurora Explorer* was involved in a major incident. The vessel was making a delivery to Dent Island near the mouth of Bute Inlet, when the master of the vessel miscalculated timing on slack water and the turn to ebb tide at Canoe Pass. As a result, the vessel became stranded high and dry. We expected her to break her back at any moment as the flotation support receded with the outgoing tide. The boat was suspended between two rocks to the extent that a person could walk underneath the hull at low tide.

The passengers and catering staff were evacuated from the ship and put up in the lodge while everyone waited for the worst. We did not expect the ship to survive but did what little we could to lessen the strain on the hull. All fresh water was pumped off and equipment on deck was moved away from the midsection of the cargo deck. For eight hours everyone watched, hoping that the ship would not collapse before the tide came in. To our surprise and great relief the vessel refloated without serious damage, but it was a very close thing.

It was about this time that Allen Dobie joined MLT. Allen and I had known each other for some time and I viewed him as a very sharp tack with boundless energy. Allen became our general manager as well as relief skipper on the *Aurora Explorer* when necessary. He stayed with us for about two years, at which point he and his wife Linda moved on so Allen could study at the Maine Marine Academy in Bangor, Maine, to earn a degree in ship management.

Allen was very capable in anything he undertook. During his term with MLT, he helped with a very delicate situation when the vessel crews wanted to organize. It was extremely difficult to negotiate a first collective agreement. There was always the possibility that an organizer from a large union would come into the picture. Had this happened, Tim and I were resigned to the fact that we would fold the company and simply go back to running the *ML#II* ourselves. Fortunately, cool heads prevailed. Tim and I could appreciate that the crews simply wanted some structure in the company and crew relations. Allen deftly stickhandled the process and after many meetings we arrived at a first collective agreement.

The unionization of our vessel personnel proved to be beneficial as the structure that it created was good for both parties. The agreement resulted in the formation of the MCMWA, the Mid-Coast Marine Workers Association. This is a full-fledged union with a registered collective agreement consistent with provincial labour standards and having all the legal force and power that resides in any collective agreement. When Tim and I sold MLT ten years later (2006) we had had only one grievance.

MANAGING GROWTH

If someone had asked me what was the most difficult part of being in business, my reply would have been managing growth. An example of this would be the timing to take on additional employees. In 1999, MLT had reached a staff level of thirty-five, including managerial and administrative staff, yard and maintenance personnel and vessel crews. This resulted in a significant payroll and ever more governmental remittances and payroll taxes. Tim and I are proud of the fact that we never missed a payroll in forty years of business.

One day we would have $100,000 in the bank account and the next day, $50. In small business one is propelled by events and circumstances, perhaps a sizeable new account or the opportunity to bring on a new revenue stream or the workload is unmanageable and relief is needed. Whatever form it takes, the minute you take on additional staff, part-time, full-time or seasonal, you probably become underutilized yourself given that someone has to train the new employee and if that employee doesn't work out then you are back to square one. All of this is overhead, and excessive overhead kills small business. Tim and I always knew that if we were not "driving the bus," so to speak, then we were pure overhead and needed to recognize that.

The *A.G. Ford* at full speed with a partial deck load of cargo entering Menzies Bay.

Tom Phillips *(l)* with an Allied Shipyard foreman. Tom was one of our stable of contractors for repair work, here with the *A.G. Ford* in dry dock at Allied's Dollarton Shipyard in North Vancouver.

Peter and Chris Thomson, founders of Trotac Marine Supply, often enjoyed coming along with me on a repositioning to or from Victoria. Part of the dedication of this book is to Peter.

The tug *Risco Warrior*, owned by Larry Heatley of Campbell River, towing the MLT barge *Coastal Roamer* loaded with heavy equipment.

The tug *Risco Warrior* (formerly *Totem,* formerly *Harold E)* tied up at Campbell River Marine Terminal at Menzies Bay. Skipper Ed Bettis *(r)* and deckhand Paul Lysne.

Chapter 9

MUCH MORE THAN JUST FREIGHT

TENDERING TO THE BC FERRY CORPORATION 1994

Our main competition in the marine freight market was Coast Ferries out of Vancouver, which had been in business for fifty years. We were aware that their main asset was a wooden coaster, the m.v. *Tyee Princess,* a traditional side-loading freighter. With roll-on/roll-off capability becoming ever more essential, such traditional deep-draught freighters were increasingly losing market share. This was due in large part to the loss of infrastructure on the coast, in the form of government docks, which left Coast Ferries at a distinct disadvantage.

Our operation from Campbell River was the more efficient "hub and spoke" structure. This meant that our market area and customers were much closer as we radiated out from the centre. On the other hand, Coast Ferries ran a linear route where their ships had to travel some distance before reaching their first customer. Departing from its base in the north arm of the Fraser River, the *Tyee Princess* would often travel the entire length of the Strait of Georgia and Johnstone Strait before coming to its first freight stop.

As previously noted, we had taken over from Coast Ferries the biweekly, year-round supply run to Whonnock Industries located in Kingcome Inlet. MLT was gaining market share, not only at the expense of Coast Ferries, but also other major carriers. This was particularly true in the central coast where we looked to expand our services into the Rivers Inlet area including communities such as Shearwater, Dawson's Landing and Duncanby and many seasonal fishing lodges.

Coast Ferries enjoyed a subsidy funded through the BC Ferry Corporation under an agreement with the Federal Government. This ensured a year-round freight service to the midcoast region of BC and was considered to be part of the extension of the federal "highway system." We were aware that difficulties had arisen between Coast Ferries and the BC Ferry Corp. but we were surprised when an invitation to tender advertisement for the midcoast service appeared in a Campbell River newspaper. Previously this had been limited to the Vancouver papers. We concluded that this tendering opportunity was directed specifically at MLT and we decided to respond.

Thus began a prolonged and protracted involvement with the BC Ferry Corporation beginning with producing a comprehensive tendering proposal. Eventually, MLT was awarded a five-year contract and an accompanying payment of subsidy.

I well remember a representative of the BC Ferry Corp. travelling from Victoria to Campbell River to "audit" our capacity to service this contract. He arrived at our Tyee Spit freight yard on a very miserable, wet and windy early spring day. I greeted this gentleman and was immediately informed that he was a "master mariner," this designation being something akin to a PhD in captaining a ship. "Ticket" qualifications such as this have never really impressed Tim or me, nor did they carry much influence with us. A "ticket" didn't necessarily ensure competency or ability to do the job. This official essentially wanted to complete the paperwork in the comfortable confines of the "office." Of course, in our case, the office consisted of the trailer parked in the yard, as previously described in chapter 4. *(p.34–35)* So it was a challenge for me to lead this individual around in the rain when his main objectives were a cup of coffee and staying dry. Over the course of the next hour I managed to tour him around our facility, finally ending in the galley of the *Aurora* where I had made sure fresh cookies and coffee were waiting. We somehow secured a favourable outcome from the visit despite the fact the official never did see the "office."

Marine Link carried out this contract for the BC Ferry Corp. for the next five years and it embroiled us in much controversy and trouble as Coast Ferries was aggrieved. At the end of the day the contract was not really worth the effort. The "subsidy" served only to skew efficiency, or the lack of, in our service to the midcoast of BC.

We did need a better office, which would include a passenger reception lounge. Again, fortune smiled on Marine Link. We purchased a small office building on Tyee Spit from International Forest Products, formerly Whonnock Industries. This office served us well until our move to Menzies Bay in 1996.

A CRUISE SHIP DISASTER

In June 1984 the cruise ship *Sundancer* (12,500 tons) struck Maude Island at Seymour Narrows. Although it was a mere three miles away, she barely made it back to the Elk Falls pulp mill dock near Campbell River. The flooded ship rolled partially onto its starboard side striking the pilings of the dock, with the result that the dock collapsed. The last passenger and crew member had left the ship only an hour before. Marine Link had the contract to load out all the recoverable passengers' baggage from the ship. Subsequently, the ship was declared a constructive total loss and was scrapped. Fortunately, there was no loss of life in this incident. Maritime disasters can happen anywhere. One needs to think of the *Costa Concordia* disaster most recently.

The stern of the *Sundancer* is resting on the bottom. Note the lifeboats have been swung out on their davits. (June 1984)

The Elk Falls pulp mill dock has collapsed.

THE A.G. FORD
A SPECTATOR BOAT FOR THE SINKING OF HMCS COLUMBIA

The *A.G. Ford* at Maude Island in the role of a viewing platform for the sinking of the HMCS *Columbia* as an artificial reef. (June 22, 1996)

Bleachers were erected on the deck of the *A.G. Ford* for people to watch the sinking of the *Columbia.* Thank you, BC Ferries, for the loan of over a hundred life jackets.

The *ML#II* alongside the *Columbia* extracting the last of the personnel before detonation.

Going, going, going . . .

Almost gone!

AIRCRAFT SALVAGE

A Cessna float plane is carefully lifted out of the water aboard *ML#I*.

The Cessna is now safely on board and away to an aviation repair facility at Tyee Spit.

A de Havilland Beaver is hoisted aboard *ML#II*.

Another Cessna is loaded aboard *Aurora Explorer.*

A SECOND INCIDENT WITH AURORA EXPLORER

By 1997 the *Aurora Explorer*'s passenger-carrying season had expanded and now extended from March to the end of October. Particularly in the spring, wildlife viewing was almost assured. Bears have just come out of hibernation and are ravenously hungry and can be seen gorging themselves on mussels and rolling over rocks to eat crabs and starfish. The *Aurora Explorer* can get close in to shore as it parallels the beach and our passengers have a front row seat to enjoy other amazing wildlife such as sea lions sunning on rocks, seals, eagles, bird rookeries and deer. A bit offshore, we often see whales (humpback, grey and orca).

Personnel on the bridge have to pay careful attention as there are navigational hazards to be aware of. A landing craft such as the *Aurora* is constructed to handle the rough and tumble of continuous beach landings. The bow is strengthened with armouring to protect the hull if a hard landing is made. This protects to a certain degree, but striking a submerged rock can be disastrous.

That is what happened on a glassy calm day in July 1997. Bute Inlet is one of the safest mainland inlets to cruise, having only a single, offshore, submerged rock in its entire length. Unbelievably, on this day the *Aurora Explorer* struck this rock, resulting in an eight-foot long gash in its hull, midships just ahead of the engine room compartment. This happened with the same captain that had previously stranded the ship at Dent Island. Fortunately, the damage did not breach the engine room and was largely confined to a single compartment.

The *Aurora* immediately made for the beach and the pumps were started but they were clearly not keeping up to the flooding. Once on the beach, the passengers were taken off over the lowered bow ramp and a call for assistance was broadcast. The cook and steward gathered up supplies that might be necessary if they had to stay on the beach for a prolonged time. With the pumps going full bore the flooding was still getting ahead. Bruce Stockand, the ship's engineer, and his son John, the deckhand on this trip, went below into the compartment that was now half flooded. Together they began jamming pillows, blankets and whatever else they could lay their hands on to stem the flow. Steadily they made progress and the pumps eventually kept up. The gash in the hull had continued slightly into a fuel tank as well but fortunately no large amount of diesel fuel was spilled.

At considerable personal risk Bruce and John had literally saved the day. Help soon came with the *ML#II* bringing additional portable pumps. A fast water taxi came to return the passengers to Campbell River before nightfall. A diver was brought in the next day and an epoxy patch was roughly fitted over the damaged hull.

With the escort of the *ML#II,* the *Aurora* made it safely back to our Menzies Bay base the following day. We immediately moved the ship to the tidal grid in Alert Bay where the hull was repaired with a temporary welded steel patch. The *Aurora Explorer* was out of service for about two weeks and three passenger trips had to be cancelled. The temporary patch held until the vessel was reconstructed some eighteen months later. *(see chapter 11)* Subsequently, the master left our employ.

TIDAL GRIDS

A tidal grid is a series of beams supported on pilings where boats of various lengths come in on high water and as the tide ebbs the vessel's keel and bottom come to rest on the cross members of the grid. Typically a tidal grid has some vertical pillars that the boat rests against to maintain an upright position on the grid. Work on the underwater surfaces of the boat and mechanical repairs to propellers and rudders take place during the low tide, typically 6–8 hours. When the tide comes in to high water and, assuming the work is complete, the boat floats off the grid. Marine Link Transportation made good use of tidal grids at Alert Bay, Campbell River and Fanny Bay.

In the winter when low-water periods are typically in the night-time hours we would work on one of our vessels with floodlights illuminating the underbody of the ship. One tidal grid that Marine Link used extensively was located at Alert Bay on Cormorant Island, opposite Port McNeill on the Vancouver Island shore. Working on a tidal grid was cost effective for MLT as we did not have to travel to a shipyard. One of the *Aurora*'s generator sets was an air-cooled Deutz diesel and this meant it could run while the ship was out of the water thus providing electrical illumination and accommodation in the ship's cabins and galley. The crew was accommodated right there on the ship and the work efficiency was maximized.

TRANSPORT CANADA INSPECTION

The *Aurora Explorer* carries overnight (berthed) passengers and therefore she undergoes a very rigorous inspection process that helps ensure safe operation. Her life-saving apparatus (life rafts, jackets, boat, etc.) are tested and inspected annually as is the sprinkler system, fire and flooding alarm system, and fire suppression system in the engine room. All fire extinguisher and signalling devices such as the vessel's EPIRB (Emergency Position Indicating Radio Beacon) and emergency handheld radios are inspected annually. Every two years the *Aurora Explorer* is hauled out of the water, usually on a marine railroad (shipyard), and her hull is inspected thoroughly by Transport Canada. All watertight hatches and doors are inspected for condition. Every four years, again while out of the water, all through-hull fittings under the water line are removed, taken apart and inspected for corrosion before being reinstalled. Every four years the vessel's rudders and propeller shafts are pulled and carefully inspected for condition.

Aurora Explorer on the tidal grid at Alert Bay. The ship is stern first to the beach and the tide is high, thus covering the grid of timbers under the hull. As the tide recedes the ship will settle on the grid and work on the hull below the waterline will recommence. The *Aurora Explorer* is in its original configuration before the reconstruction in 1998–99.

The tidal grid at Fanny Bay where the *ML#II* was repaired after its incident in Okisollo Channel; seen here at low tide. The vessel was positioned on the grid at high water and work commenced on the falling tide.

CRMT's heavy lift forklift loading building materials onto the *Aurora Explorer.* Guy Adams, on the right, is load master. Note the wood "wear deck" protecting the steel plate beneath. *(see p.112)*

Aurora Explorer working with a helicopter on a silviculture project. The helicopter lifts bags of fertilizer from the deck of the ship. Note the raised landing pad, lower centre of the photograph.

AURORA'S COOKS

If I had to choose the toughest job on the boat hands down it would be that of the cook. True, the master carries the full responsibility for the safety of everyone on board and the ultimate management of the ship in any circumstances; and the engineer is close behind making sure that all the systems throughout the ship are fully operational. However, if the cook is discontented or not up to par, then look out! because most likely it is not a happy place to be. It is a very demanding job: usually out of bed around 4 A.M. to begin the day's baking, get the coffee on and make preparations for breakfast, joined around 6:30 A.M. by the steward; mid-morning is spent prepping for lunch and supervising housekeeping and galley clean up; at noon, some days, head down for a nap and up at 3 P.M. for more baking, cooking and serving the dinner meal; and sometime around 9 P.M. head down for the night. Planning future menus, ordering supplies, co-ordinating the day's activities with the master, socializing with passengers and maybe even squeezing in an off-ship activity usually come at the expense of sleep or rest—and always done with a smile.

The *Aurora Explorer* has been, and continues to be, blessed with excellent and dedicated ladies in this position and, indeed, some stand out. Wendy Deluca was the *Aurora*'s first cook; she appears several times in the book to highlight some of the cook's duties—preparing food and setting up in the dining room, providing a barbecue on shore and, below, demonstrating creative baking skills with a birthday cake for a passenger. Donna Sawatsky stands out in my memory as one I could always count on. Shannon Brown started as a steward on the *Aurora* and is now the senior cook—very capable and a wonderful personality. Not to be overlooked is Pat Sephton who served for many years. A very great "thank you" to these ladies for creating a wonderful setting for our passengers.

Chapter 10

THE DEVELOPMENT OF CAMPBELL RIVER MARINE TERMINAL LTD.

The year was 1995. We continued operating from Tyee Spit while trying to find financing to develop our six-acre leasehold in Menzies Bay. I had come up empty except for the FBDB offer which, as noted earlier, I had decided to turn down. We still had nineteen years left on the lease with MacMillan Bloedel, but time was wasting.

One day John Hitchock of Forest & Marine phoned me. He had observed our difficulties and essentially he said, “We aren't really in the real-estate development business, but go for it.” So there we were with a green light to put nearly a million dollars into the leasehold for a new home for Marine Link Transportation. Campbell River Marine Terminal (CRMT) became a new venture and a wholly owned associated company of Marine Link Transportation.

The work got underway once winter had passed and the ground was dry enough to safely work without creating a mud hole. We had about six months of work ahead and Tim rose to the occasion, literally immersing himself in the new project, the clearing, the excavation and the construction. He contracted Uplands Excavation to do the initial clearing of the land. Once this was completed, he engaged A-Wood Bulldozing of Campbell River as the primary excavation contractor. Both George Stuart of Uplands Excavating and Alec Wood of A-Wood Bulldozing were well known for their quality work. Once the initial excavation had taken place, filling for the seaward pier began. This formed the foundation for the bulkheads and loading and unloading ramps and involved trucking in considerable quantities of blasted rock which was then pushed seaward into the bay.

A major issue was that of habitat compensation, which was mandated federally by the Department of Fisheries and Oceans. The DFO was the lead agency we dealt with for various regulatory approvals. The other agencies that signed off on the development were the Strathcona Regional District, Environment BC, BC Fish and Wildlife Branch, and Environment Canada and Navigable Waters Canada, which were both federal agencies. It was an arduous process, all governed by the policy of “no net loss of fisheries habitat.” If we dumped rock within the waterlot (which we leased from the provincial government) we were burying a section of the intertidal zone. Compensation for this involved creating new marine habitat on a two-for-one basis elsewhere.

In our case this took a variety of forms,

one of which was to go back to our old Tyee Spit base with an excavator and create benches along the river bank that would flood at high tide to enable estuary grasses to take hold. Any eel grass that would be impacted within the Menzies Bay waterlot was relocated one blade of grass at a time at huge cost and replanted in a designated area at the head of Menzies Bay. MLT also wrote a sizeable cheque to the Campbell River Conservation Society to fund further habitat reclamation in the Campbell River estuary.

Nevertheless, we had a pretty easy time with the red tape, inasmuch as this new home for MLT moved our activity out of the Campbell River estuary. This had been a long-term objective of the City of Campbell River and DFO for some time. Menzies Bay had been an industrial site since the turn of the twentieth century and our relocation there was a natural fit. In fact, CRMT is now situated where the town of Bloedel used to be in the 1920s.

Once the excavation and seaward fill were well underway, Lee Roberts and his pile-driving operation came to the fore and pilings and dolphins were driven for the vessel tie-up float system in the waterlot. Some very innovative and cost-saving measures were developed by Tim and Lee, the most significant being the construction of the sidewall pier and bulkhead system. Normally this was an interlocking sheet-steel panel, driven one panel at a time by a pile-driver, and was enormously expensive. Tim and Lee came up with the idea of using the end sections of scrapped rail flatcars to create the pier. Essentially this involved cutting off the last 15' of the railcar flatdeck at each end. These were then filled with concrete and rebar and, once the concrete had gained sufficient strength, the panel was stood on end and welded together with tiebacks to secure the structure. This resulted in a series of panels forming the vertical sheet wall, an innovation which produced a comparable system at about half the cost of a standard pile-driven sheet wall.

Our new base obviously needed a source of potable fresh water and the area surrounding Menzies Bay was well known for wells being drilled and coming up dry. MB had drilled a number of deep wells hoping to find sufficient ground water for a sprinkler system on their dryland log sort, located immediately next door. So it was with some concern that we began drilling to find a sufficient supply of fresh potable water. Tim and his practicality engaged a water witching service with the successful result that the well drilled produced a flow of twelve gallons a minute. This is not a large flow but was at least sufficient to supply our domestic needs and a water supply for vessels.

Part of the new terminal included the construction of a warehouse as well as docks and tie-up floats, all of which was undertaken by Tim and Bruce Stockand, with the close involvement of Wally Parker. Wally was a long-time customer of MLT, particularly in the Stuart Island and Sonora Island area near the mouth of Bute Inlet. Here he had been involved as a building contractor for numerous fishing lodges in that area. Wally is one of a kind, like Lee Roberts and many others whom we engaged over the years. These people are all highly productive, highly innovative, salt-of-the-earth types with whom Tim and I enjoyed working. The building of the terminal came together, under budget and on time, thanks to Tim's enormous organizational ability.

After a ribbon cutting ceremony at Menzies Bay on September 15, 1996, MLT moved from Tyee Spit.

MLT was the initial occupant of the terminal, but it was soon followed by other operations. One was Totem Transport, then owned by Larry Heatley. Totem consisted of a tug and ramp barge both of which were engaged primarily in the installation of booming grounds for logging operations throughout the Strait of Georgia, Johnstone and Queen Charlotte Straits and adjoining inlets.[1] MLT purchased the ramp barge and entered into a joint venture whereby Heatley continued to own the tug. This combination enhanced the operational efficiency of MLT and Totem Transport. CRMT was also a beneficiary, enjoying greater throughput of freight over its bulkheads and ramps. There was also additional moorage revenue.

Wally Parker.

The terminal design was well thought out. The bulkhead system is essentially a concrete wall that ramp-equipped vessels use for loading and unloading. It consists of a low water, midwater and high water bulkhead arrangement which provides all-tide access for the customer. A ramp barge and a landing craft like the *Aurora Explorer* carry their own ramp for loading and unloading purposes, so the marriage of the two, the bulkhead and the vessel ramp, is a very simple and workable arrangement. The seaward pier includes two shot rock (blasted rock) ramps graded to a 45° slope. These ramps are used for loading and unloading heavy equipment such as bulldozers and excavators. The side wall pier is the third element and is used for loading and unloading with cranes or vessel-mounted booms. The overall design and placement of bulkheads, ramps and side-to wall allows as many as five simultaneous loading or unloading operations to take place which happens occasionally at the terminal.

Since its inception, CRMT has seen a steady rise in business both from marine carriers locating as tenants at CRMT as well as other operators using the facilities on an as-needed basis. CRMT is a full-service facility and its parameters of sheltered water and efficient design have been fully proven in actual operation over the past eighteen years.

1. The area CRMT and MLT service is now known as the Salish Sea. It is the intricate network of coastal waterways that stretches from Desolation Sound at the north end of the Strait of Georgia to the south end of Puget Sound in Washington state. The waterways of the Salish Sea were important trade routes for the Coast Salish Nation. The name Salish Sea was endorsed in 2010.

CAMPBELL RIVER MARINE TERMINAL CONSTRUCTION

The six-acre Menzies Bay land has been logged and the first step is to remove the organic topsoil overburden into storage berms at the top of the property.

A substantial excavation where the first warehouse would be built.

The beginnings of the seaward pier as rock is pushed into the intertidal zone.

Another view of the expanse of the excavation.

Work continues on the seaward pier with Lee Roberts' crane assisting.

One of Alec Wood's rock trucks seen backing up with additional rock material. In the background is Lee Roberts' pile-driving barge.

An overturned end from a scrapped flatdeck railcar showing its structural steel strength underneath. Each of these ends will be half-filled with reinforced concrete and then stood up by Lee Roberts' crane and positioned to form part of the sheet-steel side-to wall dock.

The high water bulkhead with the side-to wall in place with strong backs. This wall eventually will be buried and a concrete cap poured on top. This innovative construction, using ends cut from scrapped railcars, reduced the cost of a similar pile-driven wharf made of sheet steel by 50 percent.

A significant portion of the shear side-to wall dock is seen here, erected with strong backs in place. *ML#II* is in the centre of the photo.

Another view, this time from seaward, looking in towards the pier under construction. On the right-hand side, the side-to wall dock is being installed.

The first building on the CRMT property, MLT's red warehouse (6,000 ft^2 / 557.4 m^2).

A second warehouse on the terminal grounds, built for our tenant, Marine Harvest Canada.

An aerial view of Campbell River Marine Terminal. At the top of the photo, the *Aurora Explorer* is seen loading at the bulkhead. (circa 2011)

A very busy facility from day one. Three vessels are seen at the loading dock.

Another view of a very busy terminal.

The *Aurora Explorer* and *A.G. Ford* loading cargo.

Some of MLT staff: *(l-r)* Allen Dobie, Bruce Stockand, Mike Pinch, Mike Pratt, Tom Bruigom, Tim Campbell, Ron Stevenson, Philippe Menetrier, Vic Wedel, Al Meadows, Guy Adams. (circa 1996)

CRMT warehouse yardman Rick Pelletier operating one of the many forklifts.

Chapter 11

THE RECONSTRUCTION OF THE AURORA EXPLORER 1997–1998

I immediately recognized that the superstructure and hull of the *Aurora Explorer* would lend itself very easily to expansion. *(see p.67)* After the grounding in Bute Inlet, we had to go to a shipyard to deal with the damage done to the hull so we decided to accelerate our plan to modify the *Aurora Explorer*.

I engaged the services of the naval architectural firm Marine Design Associates (MDA) of Victoria to collaborate with Tim and me to produce the design drawings and specifications necessary. These drawings would be submitted to Transport Canada Ship Safety for approval before the project could go ahead. I also engaged the consulting services of Mike Connor who was a personal friend of my father. Connor had been the lead naval architect in designing the enlargement and reconstruction of a number of BC ferries. These ships had been lengthened and a new car deck added as well as additional passenger lounges.

We also started the process of evaluating which shipyard was best able to carry out the project. It was natural that we would consider John Jenkins first because of our long-term relationship. John was able to convince Tim and me that his yard could do the work on budget and on time. The plan was to carry out the work over the winter and spring of 1997–1998.

Again, the understanding was that MLT could bring some of its own staff to work on the project. The advance fabrication of the major components began six months before the ship's arrival at the Esquimalt Graving Dock. These components consisted of a new accommodation deck that would raise the *Aurora*'s superstructure and a 45' centre section that would lengthen the hull. Sponsons would then be added port and starboard to widen the ship.

The *Aurora Explorer* arrived alongside the concrete wall at the graving dock on October 1, 1997, and work began in earnest. First up was the cutting and lifting of the old superstructure, which consisted of the wheelhouse deck and the galley deck. This was placed in the Jenkins area of the dock utilizing the 150-ton railroad crane, leaving only the engine room trunk casings on the hull. The hull of the *Aurora Explorer* was then lifted by the crane and placed on blocks on the concrete escarpment. Work began by cutting away the parts of the hull that were damaged. The bow ramp had been removed and left at CRMT where alterations would be carried out in house.

Tim had done considerable preparation ahead of leaving Menzies Bay so that when we arrived in Esquimalt work could proceed without delay. This included degassing tanks and cleaning up bilges to make the hull safe for welding and cutting. We also had to make sure that any tools we would need ourselves were loaded on board. At the end of the first month we had deconstructed the boat and were essentially left with what appeared to be just piles of cut up steel. My father visited one day at this juncture and became quite distraught by the fact that the *Aurora Explorer* no longer existed and he said he would not return until we had something that looked like a ship.

Over the next five months Tim and I literally lived in the graving dock. We had to be there because there were always decisions to be made. The MLT crew worked mainly in the engine room and accommodation sections of the ship. Even the role of chasing and purchasing parts, fittings and supplies, instead of having the Jenkins staff do it, saved us significant money.

When a vessel is taken to a shipyard you want to get value for your money—which means you have to be there. Some shipyards are excellent, such as Jenkins Marine, but they all look for "extras" to move the cost up, such as alterations away from the drawings or specification book. You have to be vigilant that your materials and supplies are actually being used on your project and not inadvertently being siphoned off by workers for another customer if multiple projects are happening on the site. At the end of each shift, Tim or I would do a walk-about and retrieve welding rods that had been left out in the elements and oxy-acetelene torches that might be run over. We also replaced burned-out light bulbs so that illumination was always available, and other such things.

By living there seven days a week we saved thousands of dollars that otherwise may have appeared on our bill. Shipyards are notorious for assigning far too many workers on a job. Tim and I were forever complaining about this and correcting it. Each day or second day Jenkins Marine controller Brian Kelly and I would check the time cards of the Jenkins workers to make sure their eight hours of billed time had actually occurred on our project. At the end of a shift "Billy" had to complete a time card for his eight hours, but two of those hours may have been sweeping the storeroom floor. The full eight hours would appear on our bill, instead of six. Also, if a second shift was needed (from four o'clock to midnight) invariably it would not be as productive as the day shift. Our presence helped to minimize much of this. This was just part of the shipyard experience.

Gradually the boat came back together, all the while being inspected on a regular basis by Transport Canada Ship Safety. Tim or I would constantly inspect all the welding by the Jenkins workers, and that of our own people, to ensure quality control.

Four months into the work saw the old superstructure, consisting of the wheelhouse and former galley and stateroom deck, being "dry fitted" to the new accommodation deck to ensure alignments and proper fit. The hull was cut transversely at midships and the two halves were pulled apart with the new 45' centre section then put in place. The prefabricated sponsons were welded to the sides of the vessel and the new bow (missing the ramp) added next. A new feature of the enlarged hull was the addition of a bow thruster which was fitted in a forward compartment and consisted of an Olympic Z-drive powered by its own engine. The propeller spun 360° which greatly enhanced vessel manoeuvrability.

The new accommodation deck consisted of six staterooms, half of which were twin single berths and the other three were of bunk-bed configuration.[1] Also integral to the new accommodation deck was a reading lounge, cook's stateroom, shower facilities and shared toilets. Since the *Aurora* started carrying passengers, there has never been a lineup for the toilets and the layout always worked very well. A greatly enlarged galley and a dining lounge featuring very large observation windows were also part of the reconstruction. Passengers have always been welcome in the wheelhouse and its new configuration included an enlarged outside observation deck with exercise bikes and lounge chairs.

Other work carried out included rebuilt Caterpillar diesel engines and realignment of the propeller shafts to enable greater clearance of the propellers from the hull thus helping to reduce vibration and cavitation in the propulsion system. All of this greatly enhanced the ship's performance, especially the increase in waterline length. This added a 20 percent improvement in the ship's speed through the water.

Now it was time to lift the lengthened hull back into the water before fitting the superstructure. This was a complicated and technically difficult procedure. Two cranes were involved: one was the 150-ton heavy-lift railroad crane on the stern of the *Aurora Explorer,* using a 4-point lift; the second was a stationary crane at the bow of the ship using a 2-point lift. As the arc of the two cranes swung over the edge of the escarpment the railroad crane needed to move forward. Everything went well and the new hull of the *Aurora Explorer* met the briny. Next, the enlarged superstructure was lifted by the crane and placed on top of the engine room trunk supports. Final fitting out took place and then it was time for sea trials. First, the reconstructed ship had to undergo a stability test conducted by Transport Canada Ship Safety which involved moving heavy weights from one side or the other of the ship and measuring how much list or "heel" occurred.

There was never any question that the *Aurora Explorer* would be stable, but the test was mandatory in any event. Casting off from the sea wall, the *Aurora Explorer* steamed toward the entrance to Esquimalt Harbour. Tim, John Jenkins and I were watching the performance of the hull and were shocked at the amount of deflection that took place in what was essentially calm water conditions. The hull flexed like a wet noodle and we knew that something was drastically wrong with the performance. So sea trials were abandoned before we even got to the harbour entrance and the *Aurora Explorer* returned to tie up at the side wall. A major recalculation was performed which mainly involved the naval architects from Marine Design and it was concluded that

1. Further modifications to the stateroom configurations were done in 2012. *(see p.166)*

the hull needed some major stiffening. The pipe railings along the length of the cargo deck were removed and were replaced by a solid steel bulwark. As well, below deck the longitudinal stringers in the hull were modified into a girder configuration. Sea trials were rescheduled and the vessel performed satisfactorily.

The *Aurora Explorer* then travelled back to Menzies Bay where the bow ramp was reinstalled and the finishing work on the interior was completed. A new timber "wear deck" was laid down at this time. This served two purposes, to protect the steel deck plate from damage, and to hold track equipment in place. Track equipment coming on and off the vessel would bite into the wood. If this wood deck, usually hemlock timbers, was not in place, steel tracks on a steel surface would be like on a skating rink.

The new passenger complement was 12 and the cargo capacity had been increased from 70 tons to 160 tons. We had a completely new ship and the vision we first had at Fort McMurray was realized.

(l-r) Wayne Clark, Al Meadows and Blaine Wright in front of the high-speed launch *Powder Hound II*. Wayne and Blaine were explosives technicians and I accompanied each of them many times, often with three or four stops a day. I was marketing Marine Link services and Wayne and Blaine were assisting logging road builders with the technical aspects of explosives.

THE RECONSTRUCTED AURORA EXPLORER

FORMER CONFIGURATION	RECONSTRUCTED CONFIGURATION
Length: 90 ft (27.4 m)	Length: 135 ft (41.1 m)
Width: 24 ft (7.3 m) in beam	Width: 34 ft (10.4 m) in beam
Passenger capacity: 8	Passenger capacity: 12
Cruising speed: 6 1/2 knot (8 mph)	Cruising speed: 7 1/2 knot (9 mph)
Cargo capacity: 70 tons	Cargo capacity: 160 tons

THE SHIPYARD WALK

Tim and I have been in business more than forty years. When you have worked together for that long you instinctively know what the other person means when he or she makes a statement that others would find puzzling. Thus when Tim and I were recently meeting in his office at the terminal and he momentarily looked out the window and exclaimed, "That guy has the shipyard walk," I immediately knew what he meant.

Although our mantra has always been to do as much of our vessel maintenance and upgrading as possible, utilizing tidal grids and in-house staff and contractors, sometimes we had no option but to go to a shipyard. In any event, the *A.G. Ford* and *Aurora Explorer* (once reconstructed) were too large for tidal grids. Although Jenkins Marine was, and still is, the best of the bunch for small vessels, we used other yards in Vancouver Harbour, Victoria and Nanaimo as well.

The "shipyard walk" essentially meant an individual was doing his/her shift or work in "bull-low gear." The worker would saunter to the work site sometime after the start of the shift, watch the clock and saunter early to the lunchroom for the coffee break and then saunter back to the work site just in time to saunter back for lunch. Actual productivity was minimal and the task took far longer to complete than it should have. These workers would also drop tools in an instant and become part of the observation gallery, apparently there to help solve "a problem" when no such help was needed.

The "shipyard walk" also manifested itself in other ways. I well remember when we were building *Marine Link #II,* Jenkins Marine would often take on workers looking to make some extra money as they came off shift from other yards. They would then work the late afternoon to midnight shift on our job, which we needed to keep up with the welding. One individual hired was exceptional both in quality of work and volume—the type of worker an employer wished there were more of. Being on site I would occasionally pick up on comments from other workers complaining that this person was "going too fast." Examples such as this continue to speak volumes about the competitiveness of our shipyard industry. Fortunately CRMT and MLT usually found good workers.

AURORA EXPLORER RECONSTRUCTION

The *Aurora Explorer* alongside the escarpment at the Esquimalt Graving Dock. The superstructure is being lifted off by the 150-ton crane at the dock.

The hull of the *Aurora Explorer,* minus the superstructure, is being lifted from the water onto the concrete escarpment and set on blocks.

The hull is blocked up in position.

The bow has been cut off and blocked up.

The hull, minus the bow, is being cut back and old steel or damaged areas of the hull are cut away and replaced with new steel.

The new accommodation deck prefabricated by Jenkins Marine.

The old superstructure, consisting of the bridge and galley levels, is married to the new accommodation deck. Marine Link employee Tom Yates is painting on the scaffolding.

Some of the MLT workers taking a break. *(l-r)* Jim McMath, Tom Yates, John Stockand and Bruce Stockand. (Dec. 1998)

The 45' long centre section prefabricated by Jenkins Marine is being lowered into position.

MLT contractor John Hurley in the propeller hatchway of the *Aurora Explorer*. John also accompanied me on a number of *ML#I* trips.

Tim and Al take a break while working on the reconstruction. *(Brian Stillings photo)*

The rebuilt bow of the *Aurora Explorer* lowered into position on the lengthened hull. The ship in the background is the ill-fated BC Ferry *Queen of the North.*

The 150-ton crane at the graving dock is moving the enlarged superstructure through "traffic" to the end of the dock where it will be dry-fitted to the hull of the *Aurora.*

The enlarged superstructure is being positioned onto the hull on top of the engine room trunk casings. This is the dry fit.

Relaunching of the *Aurora*'s hull. The heavy-lift railroad crane *(l)*, with a 4-point lifting bridle and a smaller 50-ton crane at the bow with a 2-point lifting bridle.

The enlarged superstructure, with a new passenger accommodation deck, is being lowered onto the stern of the hull which is now in the water at the side of the dock.

Back at the Menzies Bay base, MLT staff remount the bow ramp.

Initial sea trials gave us concern for the structural strength of the lengthened hull so the pipe guard rails were removed and a solid bulwark added to stiffen the ship.

Chapter 12

THE SMARTEST THING WE EVER DID

Tim and I have always had our ear to the ground looking for opportunities. The services to the forestry sector provided by Marine Link have always been the core of our business. Our major forestry customers were Interfor and Western Forest Products and their major contracted logging companies. We did a small amount of work for MacMillan Bloedel, mainly out of Port McNeill, but our major contact was now in the tenant/landlord relationship. MB had fallen on difficult times, in part due to market realities, most particularly the loss of much of the Japanese market. MB's financial malaise lay in the fact that it had drifted away from its core activities of logging and sawmilling into shipping and other ventures. This resulted in financial distress. In 1997, a hotshot "fixer" in the person of Tom Stevens, an American, was installed as CEO to turn MB around, get it profitable and get its share value back up.

Marine Link Transportation was into the sixth year of our lease with nineteen left to run. MB was clearly in a divesting mode which spelled "opportunity" to test the waters and see if the land we occupied under lease might be for sale. I placed a call to the MB property manager I had dealt with as a tenant. Control of MB properties had shifted away from its divisional offices into a centrally managed section at its headquarters on West Georgia Street in Vancouver. When I called I was informed that the property might be for sale and he would check and get back to me. The answer came back, "Yes, it is for sale." I then asked the logical follow up question: "Can we purchase more than the six-acre leasehold we currently occupy?" Again the response, "I don't know but I will get back to you." Again, the response was a positive one, resulting in our six-acre leasehold becoming a twelve-acre purchase. It took a couple of months for us to come to an agreed price and after much back and forth we came to a purchase/sale agreement. Thus began the process of subdividing this parcel of land from the greater MB landholding of District Lot 1.

At the outset of these negotiations, I was aware that MB had earlier downsized its property management staff by 50 percent. One of the casualties of this downsizing was Bob Love. As he was between jobs, I asked him if he might head up the subdivision process for our purchase. Bob agreed and what I had effectively done was hire a former MB property manager to stickhandle the complex process of subdivision and the final purchase. This worked well as the subdividing process is lengthy and technically difficult and I was greatly relieved not to have to head it up myself. The subdividing took approximately six months to complete.

Along the way, Bob brought up an interesting bit of trivia when he said, "This is a historically significant event." My quizzical look resulted in the explanation that our subdivided twelve-acre parcel was now Lot 1 of District Lot 1. In other words, District Lot 1 was the first designated district lot in the province of BC, immediately following BC's adoption of the Australian land registry system in 1885.

TIMING IS EVERYTHING

As usual, Forest & Marine had been very supportive throughout our growth and they again assisted by funding the purchase of the Menzies Bay property. When I analyzed the big picture, I was convinced that the nineteen years remaining on the lease was probably the main factor in our success in purchasing the property. Had the lease been shorter or near termination I doubt that we would have had the leverage to see the deal through. The purchase was highly advantageous to our position. We were now owners instead of tenants and we consolidated all the investment that had previously been put into the property.

Two weeks after inking the deal, MB was bought out by Weyerhauser Ltd. Looking back, I realize the purchase would not have gone forward under the new owner. Indeed, timing is everything in life.

WE BECOME A LANDLORD

We had previously developed the terminal and now we owned the property it was on. It was essential to grow our business out and attract throughput and tenant occupancy.

We had some competition in the marine terminal business from another terminal in the area that had been a federal government infrastructure project. This was Middle Point Terminal, located approximately 8 km (5 mi) north of Campbell River in Duncan Bay, near the now-defunct pulp mill at Elk Falls. It had evolved into a bulk terminal for the shipment of coal from the Quinsam Mine as well as significant shipments of scrap metal which was loaded onto barges. The design of the facility left a lot to be desired as it was wide open to southeast weather, tidal surge and had a navigational hazard known as Warspite Rock right offshore. As it was a federal project, the comment commonly made was that it was a terminal designed by a committee back in Ottawa. Many operators recognized the functionality and superiority of our design at CRMT and over time moved their operations to our terminal.

There was additional competition from a rudimentary terminal on the other side of Menzies Bay. Luckily, this property was bought up and turned into a dryland sort by Timberwest Corporation. This resulted in Inlet Navigation, an important marine transportation operator on the BC coast, moving to CRMT. Inlet Navigation is a tug and barge operation with two tugs, the *Bellisle Sound* and *Coastal Destinations,* the landing craft *Inlet Transporter,* as well as two equipment

A pen assembly for a fish farm is being put together at the terminal dock. When complete, the pen assembly will be towed away. The flotation parts are being off-loaded from the truck by crane. In the foreground is one of the terminal's shot rock ramps.

Inlet Navigation's two tug boats, the *Bellisle Sound* and *Coastal Destinations*, secured at CRMT. On the left are the ramps of Inlet's two fuel barges.

and fuel barges. Another major freight transporter that uses our terminal is North Arm Transportation of Vancouver, which services the Queen Charlotte Islands.[1]

We also built a second warehouse on the terminal property. This was a build-to-suit structure for Marine Harvest Canada for its use as a depot for the repair and storage of nets and all and sundry supplies involved in fish farming. Today Marine Harvest Canada is the major player in the BC fish farming industry.

The primary revenue stream of CRMT is throughput across the bulkheads and ramps consisting of freight of every description, both inbound and outbound. In addition, other revenue-generating services include long-term storage of heavy equipment, inventory control of boom gear and other such items, materials handling, moorage of vessels in the waterlot, docking and vessel tie-ups, warehousing and storage. Also, repair of customers' goods and equipment takes place through Ripple Rock Repairs, an affiliate of CRMT.

CRMT is a dominant piece of marine infrastructure which services the Campbell River area. It enables a large number of suppliers of goods and services to connect with customers and commercial activities in the upper Strait of Georgia and Johnstone-Queen Charlotte Straits area.

1. In 2010, the Queen Charlotte Islands group was renamed Haida Gwaii acknowledging the Haida First Nations people.

FOREST & MARINE FINANCIAL CORPORATION

Many references to Forest & Marine Financial Corp. appear in this book and I would be remiss if I failed to explain more about who and what F&M was all about. F&M was founded in July 1983 when a group of businessmen, including a number of logging contractors and friends of John Hitchcock, got together to form an alternative source, other than the large banks, of financing for logging equipment, marine vessels and small aircraft. John had begun his career in banking in the UK but early on emigrated to Canada. Beginning in Toronto with the Bank of Nova Scotia, he soon moved to BC where he held branch manager positions in three financial institutions, Wardley Canada Ltd. being one. In 1981, changes in the Bank Act allowed foreign banks to operate in Canada as Schedule B banks, these merged into the HSBC.

John eventually ended up in Nanaimo as a branch manager for Wardley where he enjoyed considerable success in financing commercial loans for forestry equipment, small aircraft and marine equipment. With this change, John found it increasingly difficult to get equipment loans approved by HSBC's head office in Vancouver. Finally, after twenty-two years with Wardley/HSBC, John resigned. A year later he formed Forest & Marine Financial Corp., with the initial investors raising $255,000 as start up capital. Interestingly, during the Mike Harcourt NDP administration in 1991, the provincial government, wishing to stimulate the economy, offered to loan F&M six million dollars in an unsecured loan which was repayable over five years on terms similar to any other

John Hitchcock, CEO and founder of Forest & Marine Financial Corporation.

David Hitchcock, chief operating officer of Forest & Marine.

investor. The government classified F&M as a merchant bank and the loan, plus about two million accrued investment interest, was later repaid in full.

To be eligible for a loan from F&M the borrower had to purchase shares in F&M to a set level depending on the size of the loan being funded. These shares were basically illiquid but an annual dividend at the time helped offset the cost of the shares. F&M helped finance this expense as part of the overall loan. During one five-year period F&M paid out over eleven million dollars in dividends. The interest rate that F&M charged on a loan was typically 2–3 percent above what the mainstream banks charged —if you could get a commercial loan from the big banks at all.

When discussing financing with other business types, I would occasionally hear comments that "F&M is expensive to borrow from." Yes, the borrower had to purchase shares, and yes, the interest rates charged on loans were higher, but take a closer look. In our case (MLT and CRMT) there were no usurious loan application fees, no personal guarantees, minimal legal costs and minimal other fees or charges. The security taken on the loan basically involved the equipment being financed and other corporate assets—not the family home. And the loan applicant got a decision in days, not weeks or months later. The "paper burden" of reporting was always reasonable, either as progress reports as the loan was drawn down, or the annual submission of the company's financial performance.

During the over eighteen years we were involved with F&M, it was always the same people that we dealt with, never a revolving door of junior account managers each wanting to "review" your file. The goal posts never moved and if we needed help because of some temporary financial circumstances then we got real assistance. I was never just a number and everyone in the F&M office knew my name, even if I couldn't remember theirs. At the end of each month I received an invoice detailing principal and interest due and we would send them a cheque. Our bank account was never raided because our payment was a day or two late.

Expensive? Not when you look at the larger picture. Over their twenty-six-year history, F&M funded 2,500 loans to about 500 customers, much of it being repeat business, such as MLT and CRMT. Those are probably 2,500 loans that would not have been funded had F&M not been there. Think of the impact that would have made on the BC economy. As noted earlier in this book, and worth saying again, Tim and I would likely not have advanced beyond the *ML#I* and *ML#II* had we not had F&M in our corner—in that I have no doubt.

When F&M went into receivership in 2009 many people got hurt financially and lost money, including the principals in F&M and clients like CRMT. Mistakes were made but it serves no purpose in resurrecting that here in these pages. Suffice it to say that I consider it a privilege to have been involved with John and David Hitchcock.

A view of the *Aurora Explorer* delivering groceries to a floating logging camp.

Chapter 13

THE SAD TALE OF THE mv TAVERNER

"You can buy a ship for a dollar and still go bankrupt." *(Al Meadows)*

With the success of the *Aurora Explorer* we began to think about possible expansion into a second passenger-carrying vessel. For a time we considered reconstructing the *A.G. Ford* to add passenger accommodation but came to the conclusion that this would require a whole new superstructure and would cost well over a million dollars. The *A.G. Ford* was proving to be an excellent freight platform and added greatly to our freight capacity. As well, the *Ford* was our main asset in fulfilling our contract with the BC Ferry Corporation and service to the midcoast.

Nevertheless, with Allen Dobie installed as general manager, MLT had the management depth and raw energy to embrace the idea of another passenger vessel within the company. For some time we had been "crunching the numbers" to determine what it would take financially to realize this ambition. In our costing analysis and business plan we needed to be aware of the IMO requirements and Transport Canada's regulatory regime.

This analysis also had confirmed that to be successful with the "pocket cruise ship" concept we would need to have a vessel that would carry a minimum of fifty passengers. Our investigation of the operating costs made it clear that a ship of any less capacity would be impractical under the heightened Transport Canada and IMO requirements. We were also very aware that as far as Marine Link Tours was concerned, retaining the freight element was imperative in the adventure cruise product. The freight was the *raison d'être* that enabled the activity of going places and seeing things. To abandon the freight and become just another cruise ship experience was not our vision. We needed to be different—and indeed the *Aurora Explorer* with its freight component set it aside very distinctly. A number of times, passengers expressed the viewpoint that "the scenery is magnificent, the food is great, the crew is exceptional—but never, never, never stop doing the freight."

Allen Dobie and I set about finding a ship that would fit this vision, one that would carry more than fifty "berthed passengers" (defined as having their own stateroom and staying overnight on the vessel) and which also had a solid freight-carrying capacity. Our search alerted us to the possibilities of a former Marine Atlantic ship that might fit our plan. This was the mv *Taverner* which had been part of the Marine

Atlantic fleet until its retirement in 1995. Marine Atlantic[1] had the vessel for sale and had tried to find a purchaser for two years without success. The *Taverner* was a 1,250-ton cargo/passenger vessel built in the early 1960s in Collingwood, Ontario, for service with Marine Atlantic. This ship began its working life sailing between Port Aux Basques, Newfoundland, and Sydney, Nova Scotia. Later, it serviced communities along the Labrador and Newfoundland coast carrying both passengers and freight. Learning it was for sale, Allen and I travelled to Port aux Basques in early 1997 to inspect and survey the vessel. We first flew from Halifax to Stephenville in Newfoundland, landing in near blizzard conditions. We were picked up by a Marine Atlantic officer who took us to Port Aux Basques where for two days we surveyed every facet of the ship.

Our inspection process gave us the view that the *Taverner,* having been a Crown corporation-owned vessel, was essentially well maintained. Her machinery and systems were dated and generally obsolete. Main propulsion was twin Fairbanks Morse model 38D8 1/8 opposing piston diesel engines, each developing 1100 horsepower and driving twin propellers. The Fairbanks power plant had been developed just before WWII for use in railroad locomotives, but the power plant found a more important calling as the engine in most US Navy submarines during the war.

This compact yet very powerful configuration had stood the test of time, but its

The Marine Atlantic ship mv *Taverner,* seen here in Newfoundland waters. This is the ship MLT tried to acquire over a period of two years and ultimately was unsuccessful. *(Marine Atlantic photo)*

1. Marine Atlantic is a federal crown corporation that provides ferry services for cars, passenger and in some cases freight, between Nova Scotia, Newfoundland and Labrador.

weakness lay in the large number of moving parts and therefore it required a high degree of maintenance. The rest of the *Taverner's* machinery and equipment was of similar vintage. The vessel's accommodation and superstructure spaces were well maintained but dated, with stall-configured shared washrooms and cafeteria-style eating facilities. A big plus was that the ship came with an extensive inventory of spare parts.

As well as its passenger accommodation, the *Taverner* had what was termed a 'tween deck cargo hold located in the midsection just ahead of the superstructure. Hydraulic winches and booms were in place on the ship to handle cargo, loading and off-loading from either side onto a pier. She was the traditional small coastal freighter which required significant shore-based infrastructure support. She featured a traditional ship's bridge, complete with a huge wood steering wheel with brass inlays, mounted in combination with a traditional binnacle and port and starboard brass engine room telegraphs. The bridge could call up slow ahead, half ahead, full ahead and astern utilizing the brass telegraph to the engine room. Both Allen and I viewed all of this as a huge asset which would draw passengers to the bridge, adding significantly to the aura of the ship.

If we were successful in purchasing the *Taverner,* our business plan entailed cosmetic upgrading of the washroom facilities to make them modern and appealing. Nevertheless, they would remain as shared facilities, similar to the *Aurora Explorer.* Additional upgrades would be done to the cafeteria, modernizing its equipment and providing a white linen dining room service. We intended to upgrade all the navigational equipment such as radar, autopilot, etc. The engine room needed some minor upgrades in terms of serviceability and safety. We also intended to fit the ship with a bow thruster to increase manoeuvrability.

Asbestos content in the ship was a major concern. It was evident in some areas of the engine room typical of ships of this vintage. Asbestos was also contained in the interior of the ship in passageway deck tile coverings and overhead ceiling tiles. Before Allen and I departed to inspect the *Taverner* we had a number of meetings with Transport Canada and came away with a tacit agreement that as long as the asbestos was not disturbed it could remain.

Our budget, including purchase, delivery to Campbell River through the Panama Canal and refitting as previously described, was $650,000 or less. We were forecasting a separate budget of $250,000 for marketing and shore staffing in year one. Our base of operation was expected to be Campbell River or Port Hardy and the ship would make five- to seven-day voyages carrying general freight to coastal communities in the Strait of Georgia, Johnstone-Queen Charlotte Straits and the central BC coast. Stops of interest and freight delivery would include communities such as Sullivan Bay, Alert Bay, Sointula, and Duncanby and Dawson's Landing in Rivers Inlet; also Namu and Shearwater in the central coast, and Klemtu, Ocean Falls and Kitimat. The ship would have an operating season of May through October in BC waters and possibly in the off-season operate in the Sea of Cortez between California and Mexico.

Our longer-term plan was based on the ship having ten to fifteen years of active service life remaining. Our intent was that this would be a springboard into a more modern ship. Our plan included the ship carrying four or five rigid-hull zodiac-type launches for taking passengers on off-boat explorations and wildlife observation. With our vision and business plan consolidated, we set about trying to purchase the vessel.

Marine Atlantic had been trying to sell the *Taverner* for two years without success. We initially offered to purchase the ship for $350,000, structured as a lease-to-purchase, with a $50,000 deposit followed by monthly lease payments. This first submission to Marine Atlantic was rejected as too low but we received no counter offer. Accordingly, we made no follow-on representations to Marine Atlantic but kept a keen eye on developments.

Nine months passed and in 1998 we decided to make a second offer to Marine Atlantic, increasing our offer to $400,000 with similar terms of lease-to-purchase. This was again rejected. We then tried to arrange an option-to-purchase with a $50,000 deposit, hoping that this would buy us some time to find additional investment. If they granted this option, Marine Atlantic also wanted us to cover their "alongside costs" (insurance, shore power, two-on-two-off watch engineers) which they claimed was around $40,000 per month. This was beyond us and no agreement was reached. With a track record of no sale in three years and no other potential purchasers we were baffled with Marine Atlantic's continued rejection of what we thought was a bona fide submission.

Our frustration level increased and I made the decision that if we could not break what appeared to be a deadlocked process then I would approach our MP for assistance. I notified Marine Atlantic of our intentions. The next thing we knew the ship had been turned over to Crown Assets Disposal. Crown Assets is the agency responsible for sale and disposal of all surplus federal government and federal crown assets. At the outset we wondered why the *Taverner* had not gone this route from day one. I confirmed that Marine Link was properly registered with Crown Assets and then awaited the bidding documents to arrive.

In due course the *Taverner* was offered for sale by Crown Assets and we made a submission to purchase the vessel for $350,000 with the required $10,000 deposit. Crown Assets mandated that any successful bid must be completed and fully paid out within ten days. Unfortunately, our position was such that we needed a thirty-day period to complete the purchase. Our submission was thrown out as a "nonconforming" bid and the sale/purchase of the vessel went to the only other bidder for $325,000.

This was a great disappointment for us, and the taxpayer of Canada took a $25,000 hit. We later learned the successful purchaser of the *Taverner* was a syndicate of Vancouver businessmen. Subsequently, the *Taverner* was brought around to the Pacific through the Panama Canal and up to Vancouver. A major refit was begun almost immediately and the intent was to convert it to a pocket cruise ship sailing the BC coast. We heard, but were never fully able to confirm, that the BC government had awarded a gambling licence to the ship.

The refit and renovation of the *Taverner*, by now renamed the *Pacific Aurora* (a play on our successful name "Aurora Explorer"), was headed up by a prominent tourism tour operator. To our knowledge, this individual had no previous experience of any kind regarding refitting a ship or heading up a project of this magnitude. Major alterations were made to the ship, the most prominent being the addition of passenger lounge capacity in the superstructure. Transport Canada Ship Safety and naval architectural involvement would need to have been an early integral part of the refit.

The *Pacific Aurora,* under the corporate name of Inside Passage Cruises, Inc., went into bankruptcy some nine months after arriving in Vancouver. The ship has been for sale ever since and has gone through a number of rebirths, including an attempt to parcel off ownership as shipboard timeshare condominiums and has to this date (2015) never set sail for any viable activity since arriving from the East Coast.

To the best of our knowledge, the *Pacific Aurora* remains under the cloud of bankruptcy and is tied up in North Vancouver at Allied Shipyard. It is a stark example of bad planning and lost opportunity.

With the *Taverner* out of the picture, we continued to cast about for a ship. Good friend Laurie McBride and I travelled to Rimouski, Quebec, on the Gaspé Peninsula, to investigate and survey another ship for sale. This was the *Echo des Mers,* but we found her not to be in sufficient condition to be of interest.

After his graduation from Maine Marine Academy, I dispatched Allen Dobie to Denmark to survey the *Disko,* a ship listed for sale in Copenhagen. This vessel proved to be of significant interest in that it was a much more modern vessel which had been engaged

The mv *Taverner,* reincarnated as the *Pacific Aurora,* tied up in the Fraser River. (circa 2009)

previously in ecotourism as a polar expedition cruise ship, travelling to the eastern Arctic and around Greenland. With the assistance of Mike Pinch and Laurie McBride a full-fledged business proposal and plan was formulated and distributed to potential investors. The *Disko* was certified to carry ninety-two passengers in forty-six modern staterooms. Our financial projections included the purchase of the ship, payment of import taxes and operational budget of 5.2 million dollars. Unfortunately, our investment proposal met with little interest and the ship was sold elsewhere.

Thus ended our lofty endeavour to bring a Canadian-flagged pocket cruise ship to BC waters.

The Danish pocket cruise ship *Disko,* which Allen Dobie surveyed in Copenhagen. Unfortunately, we were unsuccessful in securing financing to purchase the vessel.

Chapter 14

OFF THE BEATEN TRACK IN BEAUTIFUL BRITISH COLUMBIA

The following photographs were taken during our years of "exploring the working coast." They illustrate the grandeur of BC's West Coast—its rugged terrain, a sampling of wildlife and a few abandoned relics of historical interest seen on an Aurora Explorer *freight boat cruise. And snapshots of passengers and some of the friendly, hardworking* Aurora *crew.*

Knight Inlet at Cascade Head showing the huge waterfall that drops straight into the sea.

ALASKA vs BRITISH COLUMBIA

(by Al Meadows)

I have been most fortunate to have travelled widely on the BC coast and much of the coast of Alaska as well. It all started when I was a nineteen-year-old crewing as a deckhand on the Canadian Survey Ship (CSS) *Richardson*. Its epic voyage in 1967 from Victoria to Tuktoyaktuk in the Western Arctic *(see p.67–70)* was my "coming of age." My eighteen years in the fishing industry, the more than thirty years of crewing on Marine Link vessels and numerous trips on the *Powder Hound II* allow me to boast that there are not many places on the coast that I have not seen. As well, Holly and I have been on a number of "big ship" cruises, one of which was to Alaska.

This all leads to my observation that, except for the Alaska glaciers calving at tidewater, the scenic beauty and diversity of coastal British Columbia's Inside Passage far exceeds anything that Alaska has to offer. Knight Inlet is stunningly beautiful, featuring many "hanging valleys," shear rock faces rising abruptly out of the water and towering to 1500' above. The snowcapped Coast Mountain range on both sides of the inlet is the source of many waterfalls, including one at Cascade Head, about two-thirds of the way up Knight Inlet, which plunges off a rock precipice directly into the ocean 500' below. A keen observer would see mountain goats and seabird rookeries on the cliffs and black and grizzly bears in the many river estuaries that dot the shore. Bute Inlet on the mainland shore just opposite the town of Campbell River, the home base of the *Aurora Explorer,* runs a close second, as does Princess Louisa Inlet in the lower Strait of Georgia.

Yet the big cruise ship industry with its fixation on Alaska blithely sails past these wonders of our marine world. Most if not all cruise ships returning to or departing from Seattle bound for Alaska travel through Juan de Fuca Strait and then traverse the West Coast of Vancouver Island well out to sea, then through Queen Charlotte Sound and Hecate Strait before entering the inland waterways of the Alaska panhandle, just north of Prince Rupert. But not before a quick stop in Victoria, or Prince Rupert, in order to make the cruise an "international" voyage and thus avoid the dictates of the US law commonly known as the "Passenger Service Act" a variant of the Jones Act.[1] This routing also avoids the high cost of having to have two Canadian coastal pilots on board, but the main advantage (and this is the biggy) is that the cruise ship will be able to dump its black water and grey water tanks[2] while offshore, before entering Alaskan inland waterways, where the fines are stiff.

Those cruise ships departing from Vancouver bound for Alaska typically depart in the late afternoon and moderate their speed northward through the Strait of Georgia timed to arrive at Seymour Narrows precisely at slack current. During the spring and summer months this is in the late night hours with Johnstone/Queen Charlotte Straits passing by in darkness. These ships meet the dictates of the Passenger Service Act as they depart from Vancouver, but they are required to carry two Canadian coastal pilots.

1. The Jones Act is an archaic piece of US legislation dating back to the 1920s which prohibits a foreign-registered or foreign-built ship from carrying passengers on a domestic voyage between two American ports.
2. Some of the more modern cruise ships do have treatment plants to handle their waste water, but even so some discharge at sea is still necessary.

The *Aurora Explorer* gets close to the falls at Cascade Head in Knight Inlet.

The most spectacular waterfall on *Aurora Explorer*'s routing. These falls in Tribune Channel, near Bond Sound, cascade over glaciated rock and form a huge waterslide.

Washing the bow ramp and deck of the *Aurora Explorer* under a sizeable waterfall.

Lifeboat drill on the *Aurora Explorer* before departure.

A magnificent Western red cedar tree preserved by Interfor. This giant is probably over 1,000 years old. Passengers walk half a kilometre to view this spectacular specimen.

Aurora Explorer tied up at Blind Channel on West Thurlow Island, where passengers disembark to view the giant cedar tree.

One of the Helifor floating camps. *(see page 128)* On the left is the helicopter landing pad/fueling barge where the heavy-lift helicopter can be seen landed aboard. This floating camp includes a cookhouse and cafeteria, recreational facilities and accommodation for the air crew, maintenance personnel, loggers and support staff. Once the harvesting is complete in the cut block, the entire float camp will be towed to a new location. *(Helifor Industries collection)*

A twin engine Boeing Vertol 107 heavy lift helicopter is seen taking off after refueling. Note the pilot in the cockpit bubble window carefully monitoring the lift off. The primary flight control in heli-logging is so demanding that the pilot and co-pilot will change positions every hour. *Aurora Explorer* passengers frequently observe helicopter logging. *(Helifor)*

The helicopter is making a water drop to two waiting boom boats. This is one of four helicopters operated by Helifor, which is an associated company of Interfor (International Forest Products Ltd.). Heli-logging is environmentally friendly as no logging roads need to be built. The logged area is usually much smaller and only patches of prime timber are removed. All excess weight has been stripped out of this machine; there are no seats except those for the pilot and copilot and the rear ramp has also been removed. Heli-logging is brutal for wear and tear on the helicopter and a maintenance team will spend the entire night checking everything out to ensure the airworthiness before the next day's operation. This is done in the hangar and landing platform barge close at hand. This helicopter can lift 10,000 lb (4,536 kg). *(Helifor)*

Once sufficient logs have been brought out by the helicopter, a self-loading, self-dumping log barge arrives on the scene. Here a large Seaspan tug is about to get underway and tow the load of raw logs to a sorting ground where each log will be scaled for volume, species, grade and condition. *(Helifor)*

An abandoned barn and pickup at the Halliday Ranch at the head of Kingcome Inlet. Homesteaded in 1895, the property is now owned by the Nature Conservancy of Canada.

The abandoned residence on the Halliday property.

Aurora passengers exploring a beach.

A recreational stop in the Burdwood Group Conservancy. Passengers are exploring many tidal pools in the intertidal zone.

(right) Brian and Katrina Skuse are aboard the *Aurora Explorer* for their marriage ceremony. The ship is positioned in Teakerne Arm with Cassell Falls in the background.

(below) A high-speed water taxi, seen in the left lower, transported the wedding party to and from the *Aurora*.

Much logging equipment from an earlier era was abandoned in the woods, to become foliage-covered scrap metal. This steam donkey, with its huge vertical boiler, has probably been sitting there for almost a century. It is seen at one of *Aurora*'s recreational passenger stops in Bute Inlet.

The *Aurora* gets close to these pictographs for excellent viewing at the head of Kingcome Inlet.

Cliff Brown of Victoria fishing off the promenade deck of the *Aurora* while getting his exercise on one of the *Aurora*'s exercise bikes.

(above) Aurora master Ron Stevenson holding up dinner.

(right) George Turner, engineer on the *Aurora,* seen here with the day's catch. Once filleted it showed up on the passenger dinner table.

Aurora passengers gathered around the marker in Cassell Lake Provincial Park in Teakerne Arm.

One of the first crews on the *Aurora Explorer,* at the time she started carrying passengers. (*l-r*) Wendy Deluca, cook; Ted Kirk, mate; John Stockand, deckhand; Bruce Stockand, engineer; and Ron Stevenson, master. (1994)

Ron Stevenson, one of the masters on the *Aurora Explorer*, briefing passengers on the cruise and expected activity.

Master Allen Dobie going over one of the ship's navigation charts with passengers on the bridge of the *Aurora Explorer.*

Company accountant Mike Pinch in the wheelhouse of the *Aurora Explorer*, with engineer Bruce Stockand in the background.

A view of the dining room on the *Aurora Explorer*. Note the large observation windows.

(l) Chatterbox Falls in magnificent Princess Louisa Inlet. *(r)* Jenny Douglas, an early Marine Link receptionist and *Aurora Explorer* booking manager, is checking out the frozen Chatterbox Falls on a cold spring day. *(below) Aurora Explorer* passing Deep Sea Bluff close to Kingcome Inlet.

Aurora Explorer passengers at Yorke Island, a former WWII garrison protecting Johnstone Strait. This is one of the concrete bunkers that housed 6" artillery guns.

YORKE ISLAND

Yorke Island is a unique WWII historical stop, located opposite Kelsey Bay on Vancouver Island. It is near Hardwicke Island in Johnstone Strait. In 1938, with the looming clouds of war, Canada's federal government began fortifying coastal British Columbia. Union Steamship boats brought most of the material from Vancouver to Yorke Island and work began on the fort. It included magazines and other structures, with a garrison of 300–500 soldiers who manned two six-inch gun emplacements. It also had Bofor anti-aircraft gun emplacements and very powerful searchlights. When the Japanese invaded the Aleutian Islands in 1942 there was genuine concern that the Japanese fleet could invade Canada's West Coast through Johnstone Strait so this preparation was justified. The fort was abandoned in 1946. The fifty-five hectare island is now a conservancy area with BC Parks. The *Aurora Explorer* makes frequent stops here and in May and June each year it is ablaze with a host of wild-flowers. The complete story of Yorke Island can be found in a book by Catherine Marie-Gilbert, *Yorke Island, the Uncertain War.*

(right) A group photo of *Aurora* passengers with a magnificent waterfall as backdrop.

(below) Passengers invariably see wildlife when cruising on the *Aurora Explorer:* an eagle along the shore and a grizzly bear with its catch.

Sea lions have hauled out onto a rocky shore and are sunning themselves.

Passengers enjoying a barbecue on the beach in Princess Louisa Inlet. In the foreground is Wendy Deluca, cook extraordinaire. In the background, the *Aurora Explorer* is "pushing the beach." Occasionally we would have the unwanted appearance of a bear when enjoying a picnic ashore. Everyone would decamp quickly back to the safety of the boat. On one occasion, the bear actually followed everyone onto the boat and had to be chased off.

OPERATIONAL AREA OF mv AURORA EXPLORER

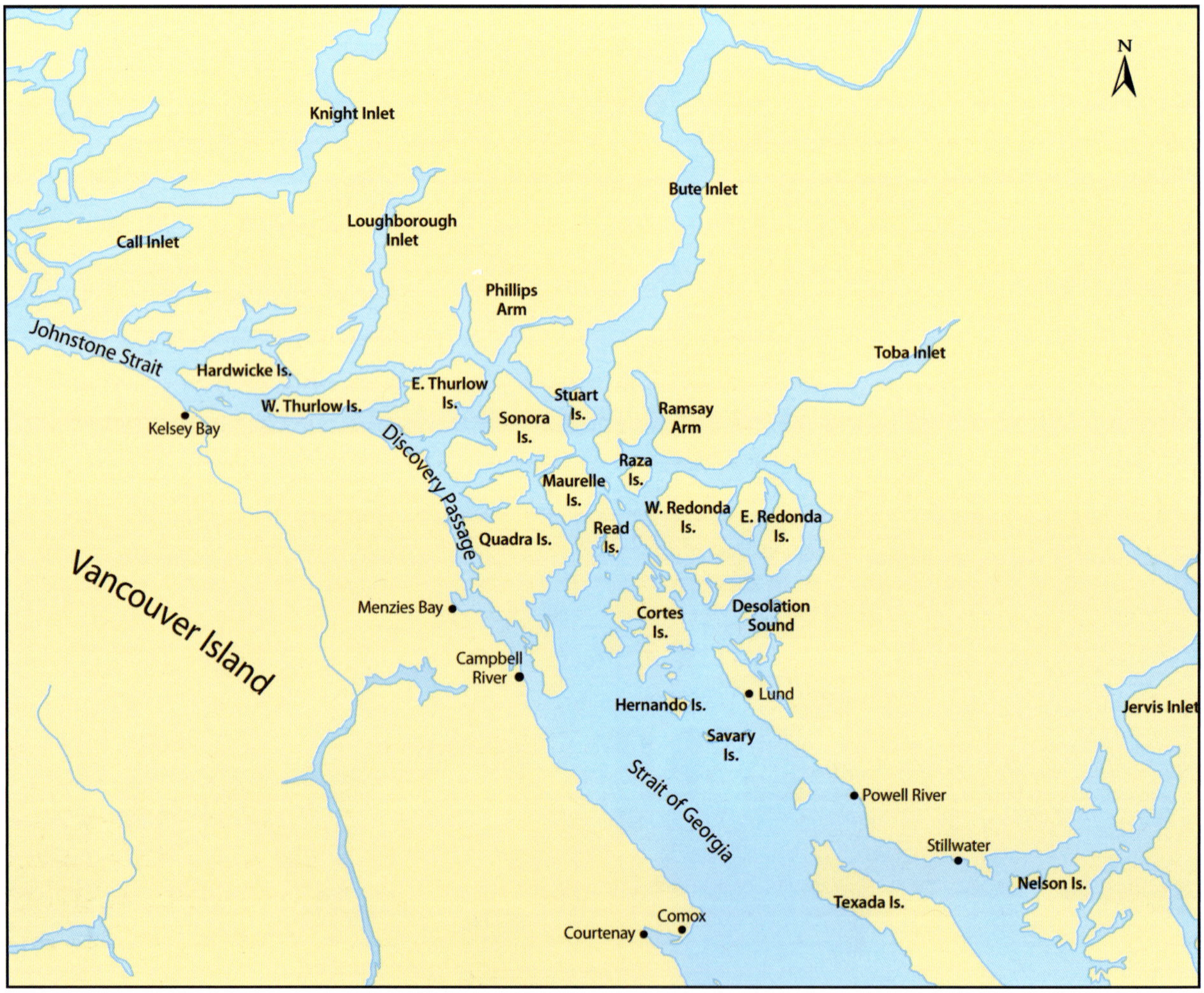

UPPER STRAIT OF GEORGIA AND CONNECTING MAINLAND INLETS

OPERATIONAL AREA OF mv AURORA EXPLORER

JOHNSTONE AND QUEEN CHARLOTTE STRAITS AND CONNECTING MAINLAND INLETS

A view of spectacular rock formations and sheer wall cliffs of Knight Inlet.

Chapter 15

A WARNING SHOT OVER THE BOW

In 2002, I was diagnosed with Parkinson's disease. It was time for me to take stock. When I left commercial fishing in 1986 I committed myself full time to Marine Link Transportation. It meant that I was away from home for considerable lengths of time as Holly and I, with our children, were still living in Victoria. There was some thought that perhaps we should relocate our household to Campbell River. Holly had a good job as a registered nurse in Victoria and her seniority would be lost if we moved.

We made the decision to stay in Victoria. My routine became one of up at three thirty, on the road by four and into Campbell River by eight for breakfast at the Beehive Cafe or Patty Joe's restaurant. After a week or ten days of working on the boats or in the freight yard I would return home for three or four days before heading back to Campbell River again. At least when I was commercial fishing I was at home for the winter and early spring months. Building the business, I was away from the family a great deal.

After our children had graduated from high school, Geoffrey occasionally served as a deckhand on the *ML#II* and the *A.G. Ford* and Andrea was a steward on the *Aurora Explorer* for one season. It was important to include my family because in the early days I had looked forward to spending time with my children on the *Lyra.* Many commercial fishermen employed their children as deckhands, an ideal opportunity for dads to bond with their children and give them summer employment. Unfortunately, I missed that as I left the fishing industry before they were old enough to come with me.

When our freight yard and operation was located on Tyee Spit and we were operating the *ML#I,* I would take the boat out for a shift of two or three days, sometimes more, or fill in for Tim in dispatch. If I was on the boat, there wasn't an accommodation problem, but if I was in dispatch I would spend the evening in the "trailer/office." Tim and I were putting in twelve-hour days sometimes seven days a week and often there was no paycheque, or at least a very small one for me, at the end of the month. I am sure many small business owners will identify with this.

Later on, when we purchased the Interfor office on the Spit, one of the rooms in that building became my home-away-from-home. Tim would do all the invoicing while out on the *ML#I* or at home. The company's business address was our Victoria home where Holly did the company books. When this became overwhelming for her, while holding down a full-time nursing position, we hired Ann Lund as our bookkeeper. When I was home I did the promotion and all the paper pushing that came with the administration.

I was often out on *ML#II*. When it was in at the dock it became my home overnight. Holly's family had a beach cottage in the Parksville area, halfway between Victoria and Campbell River, which also saved me from having to travel when road conditions were less than ideal, particularly in the winter time. Later on, when I wasn't out on the boats that frequently, we built an apartment for me in one of the warehouses.

In 2001, we hired Ford Cannon as our general manager and he lived on board his sailboat tied up at our dock. This relieved a considerable amount of my workload, which I welcomed.

Ford Cannon worked on special projects for MLT, 1995–1996, and as general manager, 2001–2003. Currently, he is MLT's dispatcher.

After graduation from Maine Marine Academy, Allen Dobie left for Charlotte, North Carolina, to work for FedNav Group. He was then transferred to Montreal where his wife Linda, a chartered accountant, had considerable difficulty finding a unilingual job in a bilingual business environment.

In mid-2003 Allen and Linda got in touch, saying they intended to move back to the West Coast to Vancouver and regain their lifestyle of sailing and skiing which they enjoyed immensely. I informed them of my diagnosis and suggested that we should talk about Allen coming back to MLT. This eventually happened and Allen joined us again as our general manager, with Linda taking over the accounting and bookkeeping as well as administration and tour bookings for the *Aurora Explorer*. Ford left Marine Link to relocate to Bowen Island, resuming his previous work as a consultant for the mining industry.

The Dobies, myself and Tim began to discuss the possibility of Allen and Linda taking over all or some of the businesses. This discussion went on for the better part of 2004, but ultimately we were not able to come to an agreement. Regrettably, Allen resigned as our general manager and left to seek work elsewhere. Linda followed a few months later after helping us train a new employee. Eventually Allen took a position with Gearbulk Shipping, an international shipping company that had headquarters in London, England.

In early 2006, Tim and I sold the Marine Link Transportation side of the business to Guy Adams, our junior partner and shareholder. At the same time, Tim and I bought out Guy's interest in Campbell River Marine Terminal. Jussi Narhi and his wife Olivia bought into CRMT and we spun off the associated business of Ripple Rock Repairs which Jussi heads up.

In the following years, my involvement in the business continued to decrease and in May 2010 we hired Gordon Littlejohn as our new general manager. He previously worked for Timberwest Corporation in land management. Gordon has continued as our general manager.

Tim and I have had a great forty-year run, which began with a call from a friend and a ubiquitous Budget hoist truck.

We have come a long way and Steve Shewchuk was right. We never looked back.

IN THE EARLY DAYS

Jack Brooks, a long-time fisheries guardian at Sooke, BC, and one of my early mentors. We are moving spawning salmon from the Sooke River into the Leech River system, with the aid of some commercial salmon troll fishermen. The photo shows the fibreglass tank in the back of Jack's truck used to move the spawning salmon above the Sooke Canyon rapids. (circa 1971)

Steve Shewchuk pointed me towards my first job in commercial fishing on the *Jean B* in 1969. He continues to be a very good friend, now a good-looking eighty-five-year-old. (2015)

FAMILY

Al and Holly Meadows. (circa 1998)

"Deckhands" on the *ML#I*: Geoffrey Meadows, age nine, and Andrea Meadows, age seven. Both were involved in the company during their teenage years, Geoffrey as a deckhand on the *ML#II* and Andrea as a steward on the *Aurora Explorer.* (circa 1987)

A SUCCESSFUL PARTNERSHIP

Tim and Al—a successful partnership and friendship lasting over forty years.

Judy and Tim Campbell. (2015)

CURRENT STAFF OF CAMPBELL RIVER MARINE TERMINAL

CRMT employees and management *(l-r)* front row: Jussi Narhi, maintenance manager and owner; Alan Meadows, president; Tim Campbell, operations manager and owner; back row: Andrew Marinus, maintenance assistant; Rick Pelletier, warehouse and yardman; Olivia Narhi, receptionist and office manager; Vic Wedel, senior warehouseman; Gordon Littlejohn, general manager; Sandy MacDonald, watchman. (Sept. 2013)

Gordon Littlejohn, the general manager of CRMT. (July 2015)

EPILOGUE

by Guy Adams

President, Marine Link Transportation Ltd.

Guy Adams, the owner of MLT. (2015)

I am pleased to have been asked by Al to contribute an epilogue to this book.

Many people will welcome this initiative by Al Meadows and Syd Heal to record the history of the *Aurora Explorer* and that of Marine Link Transportation Ltd. Very few people in the maritime community take the time or make the effort to undertake a record or legacy of important vignettes of our coast. Syd is one of the few maritime historians still working at this, and at the age of eighty-nine. I have enjoyed reading a number of Syd's books. There is a list of his titles on page 177.

In 2006, I bought MLT as well as the boat and freight end of things and it continues to be a success. Of course, the diamond in the fleet is the *Aurora Explorer.* 2014 was the *Aurora Explorer*'s twentieth full season of operation and we welcomed our 8,000th passenger. When Al created the business he also created the theme "Explore the Working Coast" for this highly successful, unique experience.

When I bought MLT from Al and Tim and other investors, they in turn bought my interest in CRMT. This transaction was totally seamless in execution and nobody lost their job or was laid off. We were all particularly proud of that.

During the changeover, I remember very clearly the short conversation I had with my accountant as I explained the deal. It went something like this:

ACCOUNTANT: "Now let me get this straight. You bought all the assets that can sink, rust, depreciate and give you gas pains with telephone calls at 2 AM, and they bought you out and held onto the dirt and the buildings? Which is more vulnerable and costly? The dirt that will be there forever, or the boat and the barges that can sink totally out of sight?"

ME: "Yeah, that about sums it up."

After purchasing MLT and the fleet of vessels, particularly the *Aurora*, we continued to polish an already polished product. Passengers who had previously travelled on the *Aurora* saw major changes, now five twin-berth staterooms and only one remaining bunk bed stateroom, work done in 2012. Additional outer shell plating on the hull was replaced. The engine room was reworked with "pod" drives on both main engines. This eliminated the tunnels in the propeller mountings, which has greatly reduced vibration in the vessel and increased its speed substantially. A great amount of work has been done toward soundproofing the night generator and we made other improvements for passenger comfort.

Of the original *Aurora Explorer* crew, the two masters, Philippe Menetrier and Ron Stevenson, continue with the company, as does Kevin Ryan, one of our mates. Bruce Stockand (engineer) retired in 2011 after eighteen years with the company and Donna Sawatsky (cook) retired in 2013 after twenty years. John Stockand moved on to another job in Duncan, BC. Jennine Chater, that voice at the end of the telephone at Marine Link Tours, remains with the company and provides exemplary service. Deb Wedel is there to provide backup support on everything. Two ladies who are indispensable.

The *Aurora Explorer* has a high number of repeat passengers, over 30 percent; some have up to fourteen trips under their belts. A new initiative is that a passenger taking a tenth trip travels at no charge. The season runs from late March through October, involving thirty-five trips, and the vessel accommodation of twelve passengers is sold out a year in advance.

This book is a wonderful legacy to Al Meadows and Tim Campbell. I extend my congratulations to them both as they move toward retirement.

Guy Adams

NOTE: For more information on Marine Link Tours see page 185.

CHECK THE FOLD-OUT MAP INSIDE THE BACK COVER

MORE OF AURORA'S KEY TEAM

Diane McCrindale, steward, now retired.

Jennine Chater, office manager, MLTours.

Shannon Brown, senior cook.

Deb Wedel, assistant manager, MLTours.

(right) The *Aurora Explorer* now has five twin-berth staterooms and a single standard stateroom that has a bunk-bed configuration. This is a typical twin berth stateroom. The second berth is to the left, out of the photo. The window looks forward onto the cargo deck. We have also made other improvements for passenger comfort.

(below) Aurora Explorer, shown here in the Esquimalt Graving Dock where Jenkins Marine is fitting pod drives. This was one of the many improvements initiated by Guy Adams. (2012)

Appendix I

A VOYAGE ON mv AURORA EXPLORER

(by Syd Heal)

Syd is an experienced seaman, businessman, writer and publisher, and an invaluable resource of West Coast maritime history—a true "ancient mariner." He took his second voyage on the Aurora Explorer *in 2009.* (Al Meadows)

On July 7, 2009, I took my second trip as a passenger aboard the mv *Aurora Explorer.* This intriguing little ship is the survivor of an epic voyage from the Arctic latitudes of Northern Canada to British Columbia's West Coast. She has been the central feature of television vignettes and articles in travel supplements.

Unlike any other passenger on this trip, I had taken an earlier voyage on the *Aurora Explorer* in 2000 so I was able to compare and judge changes and improvements. In 1997/1998, there had been a major three-dimensional reconstruction of the ship which increased the passenger capacity from eight to twelve as well as increasing the cargo capacity. I noticed improvements in every department, navigation, safety, catering and accommodation. It had been "very good" in 2000, but now I rated it "excellent." The *Aurora Explorer* went from work barge to coastal cruiser—turning a "sow's ear" into a "silk purse," as the saying goes.

The voyage began at Menzies Bay, 15 km (9 mi) north of Campbell River, BC. We left on a Tuesday evening in a light but consistent rain typical of the BC coast, which gave way in the early hours of the following morning to beautiful weather for the rest of the voyage. Soon after we were underway and through Seymour Narrows, Master Ron Stevenson left the bridge in charge of the mate as the ship headed north making for Picton Point and our first delivery of two all-terrain vehicles for a tree planting operation. He came into the dining area and addressed the passengers, giving us an outline of the planned trip: calls at Loughborough Inlet, Blind Channel, Stuart Island, Bute Inlet, Raza, Maurelle and Texada Islands, with a final call at Wesview, near Powell River.

The cargo carried was a mixed bag, consisting mainly of construction supplies for ongoing real estate developments along the coast. Logging equipment and supplies were at a minimum, although we did visit a camp in Loughborough Inlet which was run by Bendickson Logging. This company was started many years ago on Hardwicke Island, a little north of where we were, and has a history as a sizeable logging operation over several generations. The Bendickson camp was one of the few remaining shore-based operations on the coast, given the depressed state of the forest industry in 2009. For anyone with an interest in the well-being of the coastal forest industry, it was good to see an active logging show with bundled logs going into the water and being pushed around in the boom assembly ground.

This was an opportunity to watch the skill of our crew unload five large pallets of groceries for hungry loggers and a large and unwieldy looking steel bunk for holding and bundling logs. It was done by two of Marine Link's four-wheel drive forklifts, one running in reverse and the other pushing, done at a considerable speed over fairly rough ground, and then whisked out of sight up a short logging road. It called for some pretty fine judgement by the two crewmen/operators.

The company owns about ten forklifts. These two were obviously versatile in their use, either in the yard at Menzies Bay, or on board the *Aurora Explorer* or one of the ramp barges, as the needs arise. As well, the ship has a permanent smaller Toyota forklift, the same unit it carried nine years earlier. This forklift is highly maneuverable, so it is used to place cargo on deck in a position to make it easier for the bigger units to take it ashore. The generous application of mobile equipment is a feature of Marine Link's speedy, efficient operation.

The fully sprinklered superstructure is an interesting study in the best utilization of deck space. It is comprised of four decks of 1,000 ft^2 (93 m^2) each. Passengers board and leave the ship on the main deck level, which also houses refrigerated storage and workshop facilities as well as access to the engine room through two separate watertight doors. A wide breezeway between the two engine room trunks provides access to the upper deck. It also contains freezer and refrigerated storage for perishable goods which form a part of the cargo. The next deck up provides space for passenger cabins and catering crew, plus full toilet and shower facilites. Above this, on the third deck, are the dining room, galley, cook's quarters, a laundromat and handy storage for the galley. There is also a reserved table for the crew where passengers are welcome to join the crew at meal times.

The top or bridge deck is complete with wheelhouse and crew quarters for the master and engineer. The wheelhouse itself is spacious and passengers are welcome to visit so long as they do not get in the way of the navigation of the ship. The promenade deck has plenty of open air space for passengers who want to take a breather or loaf in the sun.

Below this superstructure block is the engine room where twin 250 hp Caterpillar diesel engines supply power to twin propellers. I was told that over the previous winter the ship had undergone a major refit. The engines had been rebuilt and while in dry dock "teardrop-shaped" pods had been fitted to the underneath of the engine room hull where the main engines were now mounted. This modification resulted in improved water flow into the propellers and greatly reduced vibration in the ship. In addition, this more efficient propulsion resulted in an increase in vessel speed.

Auxiliary power is provided by two generators, also situated in the engine room; one is 35 kw and the other is 25 kw. One or both of these generators provide electrical power to the entire ship, including when the vessel is tied up, humming quietly through the night.

Marine Link Transportation and the *Aurora Explorer* had come a long way since my first voyage. I was impressed by the abundance and quality of the food served on board. Pat Sephton was the cook on this shift and Donna Sawatsky, a Marine Link veteran who was the cook nine years earlier, filled in for the regular steward. In a small unique maritime business like this one, the crew has to be versatile.

Together they made a very efficient and charming team. Pat was up at 04.00 hours with coffee as the first order of business, all the while baking the day's bread. As the *Aurora Explorer* got underway, a fresh supply of cookies went into the oven for the very early risers. Hot cakes and a selection of fresh cantaloupe and melon followed. All this before the main breakfast dishes—pancakes and sausages or traditional bacon and eggs—were served at about 09.00. For the more diet-conscious, a full selection of cereals and fresh fruit was available. Lunches were basically a small smorgasbord of meats, salmon and salad items, with all the trimmings.

Dinner was the main feaure of the day and, as usual, the galley did an excellent serving. The ship's wine list featured carefully selected fine wines from Vancouver Island and Okanagan vineyards. It was obvious that the company took its cruising and passenger catering activities seriously—a sophisticated touch which did not go unnoticed or unappreciated. On the first evening, the main course featured plump breast of chicken, the second evening, halibut, and on the third it was New York strip loin steak, all prepared outdoors on the ship's oversize barbecue. To say the least, it was always a sumptuous repast.

Every passenger on board appreciated that this experience was quite different from the "gin palaces," the large cruise ships that ply the coast from Vancouver and Seattle, via Victoria, to Alaska. For those ships the BC coast is incidental and like a fine wine on an

FROM THE BRIDGE

Up on the bridge, Master Ron Stevenson and Mate Kevin Ryan calmly survey all before them with the confidence of seasoned experts. They know every rock and hazard on the route. The ship is steered by autopilot with the master or mate making adjustments in the course as they go. The traditional ship's wheel is there but is seldom touched. The ship is highly manoeuvrable in any event with twin propellers and twin rudders. Also built into the ship is a bow thruster up forward which is an effective steering assist for the ship's master in docking or coming off a beach.

unappreciative tongue those passengers miss a great deal. There is no comparison—one is a mass-produced cruise product, the other, a specialized personal experience.

The *Aurora* cruises through the myriad of islands and channels and travels up long inlets, sometimes deep into the BC interior. The weather is typically west-coast maritime at the entrance to an inlet, but at its head, so far inland, it is more typical of the interior climate, much drier and much warmer in summer. These inlets are flanked by towering snow- and glacier-covered mountains, some of the highest in North America, and cascading waterfalls. It is truly a unique experience, right in our own backyard.

We called at the Raza Island fish farm operated by Mainstream Salmon on the way into Bute Inlet. Next we visited Marble Bay on Texada Island to deliver a large truck. We laid over there for an overnight rest, a Transport Canada requirement. Then we were on our way to Westview to deliver dangerous goods, in this case six tons of explosives for the limestone quarries on Texada Island. It was all handled safely and expertly.

The last leg of the voyage from Powell River back to Menzies Bay was like a long and pleasant toboggan ride in the open ocean. The weather and sea conditions were perfect and even some seagulls agreed with this as they perched on the upper edge of the bow ramp.

As we neared the home port of Menzies Bay under ideal conditions I thought of the history of the *Aurora Explorer* and the ship's owner Marine Link Transportation. MLT's advertising motto is "Explore the Working Coast" as the *Aurora Explorer* takes its passengers off the beaten track—adventure cruising. It explores the endless waterways of the BC coast and picks up and delivers cargo in places that seem to have no name and little in the way of a dock, ramp or even a proper harbour. Passengers are witness to things that are completely out of the realm of their everyday lives. For many of us on that trip it was a once-in-a-lifetime experience.

A group photograph of the crew and passengers at the Burdwood Group Conservancy, before reconstruction of the *Aurora Explorer.* My mom, Hilda, is seated on the right and my father, Dick, behind her.

Crew and passengers on the beach at Hernando Island. The ship is post reconstruction.

Aurora Explorer with the ramp down at Rebecca Spit on Quadra Island "pushing the beach." The passengers are off exploring on shore.

Aurora Explorer underway in Johnstone Strait.

Appendix II
IN THE WAKE OF THE EXPLORERS
by S.C. Heal

Not everyone shares an interest in history, so this section is added for the benefit of those who do. Personally, I have a deep interest in the subject to the point that most of my writing over the past twenty-five years has a historical basis.

Today, the area served by Marine Link Transportation and cruised by the *Aurora Explorer* is the Northern Gulf Islands and the mainland inlets from Jervis Inlet, as far north as the complex of inlets known as the Seymours, a little north of the north end of Vancouver Island.

The area served is steeped in history, starting with the unproven proposition that Sir Francis Drake, circumnavigator of the world, was in these waters in the sixteenth century.[1] Early Spanish explorers worked their way north from Mexico and what is known today as California. At about the same time the English naval captain James Cook sighted the entrance to the Strait of Juan de Fuca in 1778 and spent a month at Nootka, on the West Coast of Vancouver Island, watering and repairing his ships before continuing his great voyage of exploration. Cook's name went down in history as one of England's greatest explorers.

The Spanish explorers Juan Francisco Bodega y Quadra, Jose Narvaez,[2] Cayetano Valdez and Dionysio Alcala-Galiano, whose names remain prominent on islands or other geographical points on the BC coast, carried on considerable exploration of the BC coast in the early 1790s. It was while they were so engaged that Captain George Vancouver of the Royal Navy met up with Quadra off Spanish Banks in English Bay which is now encircled by the modern City of Vancouver and the Municipality of West Vancouver.

George Vancouver arrived on the coast in 1792 with his ships HMS *Discovery* and HMS *Chatham*. Of all the explorers he made the greatest contribution. His detailed maps and charts proved to be extraordinarily accurate and comprehensive, but his place in

1. This claim is made, with some evidence to back it up, in Sam Bawlf's controversial *The Secret Voyage of Sir Francis Drake*. Some historians dispute Bawlf's claims, dismissing them as conjecture.
2. Narvaez was the commanding officer based at Nootka; he dispatched his two lieutenants, Valdez and Galiano, to explore the Strait of Georgia and the Gulf Islands. In 1805, Valdez and Galiano were at the battle of Trafalgar in command of Spanish ships, part of the line which was decimated by Nelson's fleet. Valdez lost his life in the battle and Galiano was taken prisoner following surrender of his ship to the British victors. Valdez and Galiano Islands are named for them.

history was marred by an incident involving Thomas Pitt, a mid-shipman and nephew of the famous William Pitt, the British prime minister at the time, who had shipped out as crew. Young Pitt was flogged by Vancouver for insubordination and shipped home to England in disgrace. Upon his arrival back in England he learned the title Lord Camelford had been bestowed upon him. With his new-found political power, he set out to stir up much resentment against Vancouver and, as a result, much of Vancouver's research was destroyed.

George Vancouver endured great turmoil in his final years, the victim of political influence, class distinction and slander which relegated him to an undeserved lesser place in the rolls of the great explorers of his era. While Vancouver's memory is much respected and even revered in British Columbia, his native land treated him shabbily, barely remembering him for the outstanding scientific explorer that he became. The Vancouver family originated in the Dutch town of Couverden and moved to England in the previous century. The Dutch treat his memory with considerable respect given his ancestry.

Vancouver was a contemporary of the great fighting Admiral Horatio Nelson, victor at the Battles of Copenhagen, the Nile and Trafalgar. Both were born in 1757, but their paths through naval service took different routes. Vancouver served as a midshipman under Captain James Cook on his memorable world-girdling cruise which renewed the British Navy's interest in the West Coast, over 200 years after Drake's visit to this general area. Vancouver did see wartime battle first hand, being present as a lieutenant under Rodney at the Battle of the Saintes in the West Indies, serving directly under Captain, later Admiral, Alan Gardner, who is remembered by Mount Gardner on Bowen Island. Gardner's patronage advanced Vancouver's career on his later scientific course that brought him to the Pacific Coast in command of his own expedition in 1792. Vancouver suffered ill health and died in 1798 at the early age of forty-one.

George Vancouver left his imprint on the Campbell River area. He sailed through Discovery Passage, which he named for his ship (and Cook's before him), on Campbell River's front doorstep. He gave the name of Zachary Mudge, one of his lieutenants, to sometimes infamous Cape Mudge which is opposite Campbell River. This has been the site of some shipwrecks in the past due to the strong tidal action which, when combined with bad weather, can stir up a nasty witch's brew of extreme conditions.

Vancouver and Quadra became good friends and, honouring this, Vancouver conferred their two names jointly on "Quadra and Vancouver Island." The name was unwieldy and "Quadra" and "Vancouver" were later separated and this large island was renamed Vancouver Island, while the much smaller island opposite Campbell River was named Quadra Island. Menzies Bay, where MLT and the *Aurora Explorer* are based, is named for Dr. Archibald Menzies, botanist and ship's surgeon with the Vancouver expedition.

Vancouver's voyages along the BC coast were undertaken over a period of four years from spring to fall in each year. His expedition overwintered at the Sandwich Islands (known today as Hawaii), which established a historic link between those islands and the future British Columbia. For some time during the nineteenth century, native Hawaiians settled in BC and their descendants have long since integrated into the Canadian population. Researchers have noted many connections between citizens of BC and the original Hawaiian immigrants.

No discussion of this coastal area and its history would be complete without mention of the First Nations people, "first" as they were the original occupants of these lands and waters. The Coast Salish people lived by fishing and hunting and used cedar and its bark to make clothes and provide shelter. They often moved on a seasonal basis to take advantage of the cyclical nature of the fisheries. They knew that the inflow of salmon and herring were related and followed the cycles so that rich hauls could be made at the appropriate time of year. One important fish was the oolichan, highly prized for its oil and also used as a source of light when dried, strung on a wick and burned as a candle.

In this area, the waterways now referred to as the Salish Sea, there were none of the major wars such as those in the United States as the Americans won their West. Perhaps the most serious event was in 1864. A business promoter/developer in Victoria, Alfred Waddington, had a bold, and now infamous, plan to build a faster route to the Cariboo goldfields. He sought to establish a port at the head of Bute Inlet and then build a "gold road" from the mouth of the Klinaklina River, into the Homathko River Valley and on to Barkerville. He sent a crew to survey and build the wagon road. The Chilcotin people resented the presence of the surveyors, fearing both infringement on their territory and the increased threat of smallpox, an epidemic that had already killed many of their people. They attacked one of Waddington's work camps and fourteen road construction workers were killed. By year end, the death toll was nineteen plus four aboriginals. Five Tsilhqot'in (Chilcotin) were sentenced to death by Judge Matthew Begbie and then hanged at Quesnellemouth, now Quesnel. A sixth man was later hanged in New Westminster.

The Chilcotin War,[3] as it became known, remained a divisive racial issue in BC for more than a century even as the province took steps to address what the Tsilhqot'in perceive to be grievous wrongs. In 1993, the BC government issued an apology for the territorial infringements of Waddington's men as well as the procedural shortcomings of the trial and hangings. In 2014 a second government went further, apologizing for the wrongful hanging of the six war chiefs. The names of Mount Waddington, the highest mountain totally within BC's boundaries, and Waddington Harbour at the head of Bute Inlet are sobering reminders of this war.

Waddington's Road was never completed because of the war. A few years later, it was examined as one of the possible routings for the mainline of the Canadian Pacific Railway. Waddington's dream was to build a railway that would bypass the lower mainland and pass down Bute Inlet. Then a series of island-hopping bridges via Cortes and Quadra Islands would reach Vancouver Island by crossing Discovery Passage near Campbell River. The railway line would then proceed down the island to Victoria. His

3. Chilcotin War details are based on information in *Wikipedia* and *ABC Bookworld Wikipedia of Literature*.

purpose was to secure Victoria as Canada's west-coast seaport and major metropolis. Unfortunately for him, the CPR chose Burrard Inlet and the subsequent development of the seaport of Vancouver.

Since the 1880s, much of the entire area has been extensively logged and, in some instances, many logging sites have been logged for second-growth and even third-growth timber. The logger and fisherman were often the explorers who followed the extensive surveys done during the nineteenth century by Captains Pender, Richards and Walbran of the British Royal Navy. They continued the work begun by George Vancouver and the Spanish explorers.

Vancouver started the naming process, and Captain Richards and his successors continued it. Howe Sound and Jervis Inlet are generously endowed with British navy names of ships and personnel prominent at such battles as Ushant, "The Glorious First of June" and Cape St. Vincent. Beyond those inlets, the navy names become thinner but persist all up the coast of BC, interspersed with many Spanish and First Nations names courtesy of those early surveyors.

The entire coast is a treasure trove of names representing a pageant of BC history. More names were added later that relate to Canadian history and personalities.

In 2014, Syd Heal was recognized by the *Nauticapedia*. John M. MacFarlane had this to say about him: "In my opinion there is no finer interpreter of the marine scene in British Columbia. He leads the pack in his general commercial knowledge, not only historically but also in a far broader field from marine insurance and finance through to practical ship economics and operations."

In 2015, Syd was honoured with the SS Beaver Medal for Maritime Excellence by the Maritime Museum of BC.

Syd is the founder and owner of Cordillera Books. He is a prolific author of marine books about West Coast BC, listed on the opposite page. *(Jane McIvor photo)*

S.C. Heal books now unavailable due to the passing of S.C.Heal

MARINE BOOKS BY S.C. HEAL

TUGBOAT INDUSTRY

FULL LINE, FULL AWAY: A Towboat Master's Story 2nd ed. *(with J.E. Wilson)*
BOOMSTICKS & TOWLINES: Logging and Water Transport: Tugs, Brokers, Rafts and Barges (West Coast Maritime Series #1)
ALWAYS READY: Tugboats Along the Coast: The Evolution of an Industry (WCMS #2)
TYING THE KNOT: Consolidations and Mergers: In the B.C. Coast Forest Companies and theTug and Barge Industry (WCMS #3)
SHOWING THE FLAG: The West Coast Tug and Barge Industry: Offshore and Overseas Operations (WCMS#4)
THE LOG SHIPS: The Story of the World's Only Two Self-Loading, Self-Propelled, Self-Dumping Bulk Log Carrier Ships
THE LOG BARGES: The Story of a Unique British Columbia Maritime Innovation
THE LOOSE CANNON: From Deckhand to Captain to the Executive Suite

DEEP SEA SHIPPING

CONCEIVED IN WAR, BORN IN PEACE: Canada's Deep Sea Merchant Marine
ACROSS FAR DISTANT HORIZONS: The Life & Times of a Canadian Master Mariner
A GREAT FLEET OF SHIPS: The Canadian Forts & Parks
UGLY DUCKLINGS: Japan's WW II Liberty Type Standard Freighters
INBOUND TO VANCOUVER: B.C.'s Offshore Trade and Ocean Shipping 1850–1945 (WCMS#5)
OUTBOUND FROM VANCOUVER: B.C.'s Offshore Trade and Ocean Shipping: 1945 to Present Era (WCMS#6)
CANADIAN CAPERS: A Seaman's Account of Voyages And Intrigues Through the Corporate Jungle *(with Svein Stokke)*

GENERAL MARINE AND TRAVEL

THE MAPLE LEAF AFLOAT (Vol. 1): West Coast Maritime Memories
THE MAPLE LEAF AFLOAT (Vol. 2): More Maritime Memories
A SOUTH ASIAN ODYSSEY: Voyages and Travels in the Last Days of the British Raj
THE ROMANCE OF HISTORIC NAMES: In Vancouver Harbour, Howe Sound and Jervis Inlet
FERRIES WEST: A West Coast Photo Album (WCMS#7)

FISHING INDUSTRY

STAND BY, LET 'ER GO: The Gillnetter Years: The Memoirs of a Commercial Fisherman *(with Robert Karliner)*

A GLOSSARY OF TERMS

ABS: American Bureau of Shipping.

ARTICULATED: Describes a piece of equipment that has a centre pin by which the machine can bend and therefore becomes much more manoeuvrable.

AWOL: Absent without leave.

BCP: British Columbia Packers Ltd.

BEAM: The width of a vessel from deck edge to opposite deck edge at its widest point.

BERTHED PASSENGER: Passenger aboard a ship who has a booked stateroom and sleeps overnight on the vessel.

BINNACLE: A built-in housing for a ship's compass, usually at the bridge steering station.

BLACKWATER: Waste water that contains sewage.

BO'SUN: A person in charge of a vessel's deck including personnel and equipment.

BOW CLEAT: A strong point attachment mounted on a ship's bow or anchor winch for securing tie-up ropes or cable.

BOW RAMP: A type of drawbridge or movable bridge that is lowered or raised to load and unload vessels.

BOW THRUSTER: A bow thruster is usually a transversal propulsion device built into, or mounted to, the bow of a ship or larger boat to make it more manoeuvrable.

BRAILER: A stiff frame usually made of aluminum fashioned to accommodate a large dip net for the purposes of landing fish.

BRINY: Saltwater; the ocean.

CCG: Canadian Coast Guard.

CHECKERS: Partitioned deck spaces where fish coming up on the gear are landed aboard.

CHINE: The bottom of the hull along the entire outer length of the vessel where the side plating meets the bottom plating.

COASTER: A term to describe a small vessel that travels the coast making frequent stops.

COMBING: A raised border around a ship's deck hatch serving to support the hatch cover and avoid flooding.

CONSTRUCTIVE TOTAL LOSS: Where a damaged object (house, vehicle, vessel, etc.) is deemed uneconomic to repair; where such repairs, if carried out, would exceed the end value of the object.

CRMT: Campbell River Marine Terminal

CYA MODE: Cover-your-ass mode

DAVIT: An apparatus intended to swing lifeboats, workboats, etc., out from the side of a ship and then lower them into the water. Usually one of a pair.

DECKHEAD: The ceiling in a ship's interior space.

DECONSTRUCT: The taking apart or scrapping of an object.

DEFLECTION: The angle of movement from the center line, either vertically or horizontally.

DFO: Federal Department of Fisheries and Oceans.

DEGASSING: The process of removing toxic gasses and making spaces or tanks safe for entry.

DEWATERING: Removing from the water; from the ocean.

DOLPHIN: A group of three or more pilings which forms a strong point in a dock or float system.

DRAFT (DRAUGHT): The depth of a vessel measured from its water line to the bottom of its keel at its deepest point.

DRUM SEINER: A larger vessel with a crew of five or six that has the distinctive feature of a large metal drum at its stern. A seine is a fishing net that hangs vertically in the water with its bottom edge held down by weights and its top edge buoyed by floats. Seine nets can be deployed from shore as a beach seine, or from a boat. The seine net encircles the target school of fish and then "purses up," much like the drawstring in a bag.

DRY FIT: When two large objects are meant to fit together and where tolerance is very low and tight, shipbuilders will often do what is known as a "dry fit." Two pieces are brought together on dry land and slowly fitted together. Neither part moves independently of the other part, thus allowing cutting and wedging. Therefore the two are married together relatively simply. Conversely, when the hull is in the water and a major part is being fitted to it, even the slightest wave action will move the hull independent of the other large part coming together as one, creating difficulty. If a good "dry fit" has taken place, only minor cutting will be necessary in what is known as the "wet fit" which is the final coming together.

DRYLAND SORT: Usually a large level space at the shoreline having either a concrete or asphalt surface where logs are off-loaded and spread out in the yard for grading by species and value.

ESCARPMENT: Concrete or asphalt surface immediately adjacent to a dock or bulkhead.

FATHOM: A unit of measurement equal to 6 ft (1.8 m), usually referring to water depth.

FBDB: Federal Business Development Bank.

FOLLOWING WIND: A condition where the wind is at your back or on the stern of the vessel.

FLUSH DECK: A deck configuration whereby all hatches are level with the deck and has no combing.

FREEBOARD: The distance vertically between the water level and the edge of a vessel or barge's deck edge.

GEN SET: The combination of an electrical generator and an engine (the prime mover) mounted together to form a single piece of equipment. This combination is also called an engine generator set. In many contexts, the engine is taken for granted and the combined unit is simply called a generator.

GILLNET: A fishing net set vertically in the water so that fish swimming into it are entangled in its mesh by the gills.

GRAVING DOCK: A dry dock; a large dock from which water can be pumped out; used for building ships or for repairing a ship below its waterline.

GREY WATER: Discharged waste water from non-sewage sources, i.e., showers, wash basins, laundry and kitchen.

HAIDA GWAII: The former Queen Charlotte Islands.

Hanging Valley: A valley between peaks that does not reach the shoreline, but rather ends at some elevation above tidewater.

Highliner: A top producer amongst fishermen.

Hot Loading: Where the delivery truck meets the vessel and off-loads directly without the use of any materials handling equipment.

IMO: International Maritime Organization.

Jog: Where a vessel moves slowly ahead, holding position in heavy seas.

Keel: The longitudinal structure along the centre line at the bottom of a vessel's hull, on which the rest of the hull is built.

Knot: A measurement of speed based on the nautical mile. One knot of speed is approximately 1.2 mph.

Leachate: Any liquid that, in passing through matter, extracts solutes, suspended solids or any other component of the substance through which it has passed. In the narrow environmental context leachate is therefore any liquid material that drains from land or a stockpiled substance and contains significantly elevated concentrations of undesirable material derived from the material that it has passed through.

Leads: Observed openings in floating sea ice, whereby a vessel can continue under way.

Lee: Shelter that a vessel seeks behind an object or point of land.

Lifting Bridles: Rigging as in wire cable, chain or rope, configured to provide a means of lifting an object with two or more points of contact.

Lifting Lugs: Strong point attachments for enabling lifting or pulling of an object.

MB: MacMillan Bloedel Ltd.

Master: Captain of a ship or "skipper."

Mariculture: Farming of shellfish.

May Day: The internationally recognized signal that a vessel or plane is in distress and requires immediate assistance.

Microns: Measurement in thousands.

Midships: The centre point on a ship's deck, equal distance from bow or stern. Also a situation where the steering rudder is straight in line with the ship's bow.

MLT: Marine Link Transportation.

Nautical Mile: 6,000 ft (1828.8 m).

NWT: Northwest Territories.

Passageway: An interior corridor of a ship.

Piling: A single treated wood pole or steel pipe driven into the substrate of a waterlot or marina for the purpose of securing a vessel float tie up (moorage) in position.

Pike Pole: An aluminum pole, 6'–15' long, having a hook on one end, used to retrieve ropes and other objects from the dock or water.

Plotter: An electronic display device which shows the track of a ship. It can also be an instrument as a protractor for plotting lines and measuring angles on a chart.

Pod Propulsion: Teardrop-shaped "pods" are fitted on the underneath of the hull. The main engines are mounted inside the pod and are open to the engine room. Each engine drives a propeller mounted on the outside of the pod. This improves the efficiency of water flowing through the propeller and thus reduces vibration and improves the speed of the vessel.

Queen Charlotte Islands: Renamed Haida Gwaii in 2010.

Radar: Radio Detection and Ranging, a primary electronic navigation and detection device.

Repeater: A telephone system repeater (to relay telephone or telegraph traffic).

Roll On/Roll Off (sometimes referred to as "ro-ro"): The capability of a ship, ferry or barge to roll equipment or vehicles on and off the vessel.

Scantlings: Scantling length is a distance slightly less than the waterline length of a ship, and generally less than the overall length of a ship. In the ABS rules for building and classing steel vessels, it is defined as the distance on the summer load line from the fore side of the stem to the centre line of the rudder stock.

Shell Plating: The outermost structure, or skin, on the hull of a steel or aluminum ship or boat. It is the structural element that renders the hull watertight.

Shipwright: A shipbuilder or a ship's carpenter.

Shot Rock: Blasted rock.

Side-To: Parallel to a wall or dock when tied up.

Skeins: The female roe sacs, light yellow or white in colour, approximately 4½" long.

Skiff: A flat bottom open boat of shallow draft, having either a pointed or squared-off bow and a square stern. Usually propelled by oars, sail or motor.

Smolts: Young salmon (or trout) after the fingerling stage, when they become silvery and migrate to the sea for the first time.

Sponsons: Structures that increase the beam of a boat or ship to increase flotation and rigidity in the main hull. Typically sponsons are added to a vessel to improve stability particularly when cargo is being lifted on or off the main deck. They can be of various designs.

Stranded: Where a vessel or barge becomes stuck on the shore or a submerged rock.

Stringers: The longitudinal parts of a hull's structural skeleton.

Strongback: A run back to an anchor point for the purpose of providing added support and security to a structure.

Tidewater: The ocean where tidal influence is present.

Trimmed: A situation where a ship or barge is loaded such that the draft at the bow and stern are set at predetermined levels.

'Tween Deck Cargo Hold: The typical cargo hold configuration where cargo is stored at multi-levels in the ship's interior decks. A large hatch opening is fitted above the hold and permits loading and unloading.

USCG: United States Coast Guard.

Void: A compartment in a vessel, usually completely empty, and in some cases designed for flotation and/or damage control as in "collision void."

Water Witching: A practice where some individuals can detect groundwater with the assistance of a forked branch taken from a willow tree.

INDEX

RECOMMENDED CRUISING OF THE INSIDE PASSAGE AND THE WEST COAST OF VANCOUVER ISLAND

If you want to see some of West Coast Vancouver Island up close I suggest the *Uchuk III* based out of Gold River. It is a small coastal freighter that makes stops at Tahsis, Esperanza, Zeballos; a two-day trip includes the village of Kyuquot.

Operated by Nootka Sound Services — 250-283-2515 — www.campbellriverchamber.ca

OR mv *Francis Barkley* based out of Port Alberni. It travels down the Alberni Canal with stops including Bamfield, the Broken Islands in Barkley Sound and the town of Ucluelet.

Operated by Lady Rose Charter Marine Services — www.ladyrosemarine.com

If you want to travel the true Inside Passage I recommend a trip with BC Ferries on the mv *Northern Expedition* between Port Hardy and Prince Rupert:

— http://www.bcferries.com/schedules/inside/ip-current.php

OR theAlaska State Ferries out of Bellingham, WA, to Prince Rupert — www.dot.state.ak.us

And if you really want to get off the beaten track, then of course the *Aurora Explorer* is the ultimate experience of BC's West Coast and the only ship carrying berthed passengers on multi-day voyages. In my opinion, the best time to go is either June, when daylight hours are longest and wildlife is abundant, or in September, particularly at the full moon when it is stunningly beautiful at the head of many inlets. Here are three videos to check out the *Aurora Explorer* experience:

— https://www.youtube.com/watch?v=CISkLWbXPqg
— https://www.youtube.com/watch?v=7yVDg1-mdb0
— https://vimeo.com/36198350

250-286-3347
info@marinelinktours.com
www.marinelinktours.com

RECOMMENDED READING FOR BACKGROUND TO THE BC FISHING INDUSTRY

STILL FISHIN': The BC Fishing Industry Revisited. Allan Haig-Brown. Harbour Publishing.

LEGACY IN WOOD: The Wahl Family Boat Builders. Ryan Wahl. Harbour Publishing.

DEAD FISH AND FAT CATS: A No-Nonsense Journey Through Our Dysfunctional Fishing Industry. Eric Wickham. Granville Island Publishing.

FISHING WITH JOHN. Edith Iglauer. Harbour Publishing.

SALMON: OUR HERITAGE. Cicely Lyons. J.S. Marshall & Co. (for BC Packers Ltd.) out-of-print

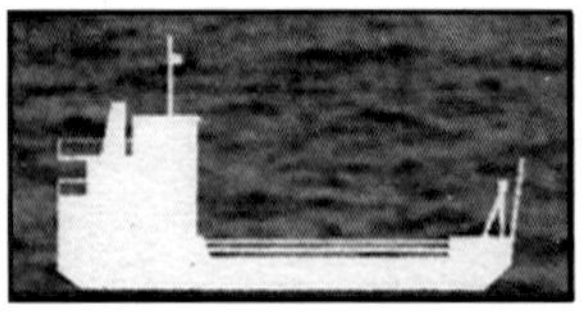

CHECK THE FOLD-OUT MAP INSIDE THE BACK COVER

“AURORA FALLS” IN BUTE INLET, BC

Point Barrow
Chukchi Sea
Russia
Alaska
Bering
Strait
Bering Sea
Kodiak
Island
Gulf of Alaska
Dutch
Harbour
Unimak Pass
Aleutian Islands
THE
DELIVERY VOYAGE OF THE
M.V. Aurora
Explorer
NINETY-DAYS
1990

Beaufort Sea
Tuktoyaktuk
Inuvik
Aklavik
Mackenzie River
Norman Wells
Great Bear Lake
Mackenzie River
Yukon Territories
Great Slave Lake
Hay River
Fort Smith
portage vessel 24 km
Slave River
Lake Athabasca
Athabasca River
Fort McMurray
Clearwater River
Alberta
British Columbia
Juneau
Prince Rupert
Edmonton
Queen Charlotte Islands
Queen Charlotte Sound
Port Hardy
Campbell River
Vancouver Island
MAP BY DENTON PENDERGAST

M.V. Aurora Explorer
AURORA EXPLORER